Prepare the Way

Daily Meditations *for* Advent *and* Lent

Prepare the Way

R. Mark Liebenow

United Church Press
Cleveland, Ohio

United Church Press, Cleveland, Ohio 44115

© 1999 by R. Mark Liebenow

Printed in the United States of America on acid-free paper

04 03 02 01 00 99   5 4 3 2 1

Library of Congress Cataloging-in-Publication Data

Liebenow, R. Mark (Ronald Mark), 1953–
    Prepare the way : daily meditations for Advent and Lent / R. Mark Liebenow.
        p. cm.
    Includes indexes.
    ISBN 0-8298-1351-9 (pbk. : alk. paper)
        1. Advent Meditations.   2. Christmas Meditations.   3. Lent Meditations.
    I. Title.
    BV40.L54   1999
    242'.332—dc21   99-41004
                                                                  CIP

———

There are few people I've met who have a knack for putting a great deal of meaning into just a few words. A. Stanley MacNair was one who was able to do this. He'd say what he had to say in a few well-chosen and articulate paragraphs and then stop, leaving one to meditate on all the worlds his words had opened up to view. His inspiration has guided me in writing this book.

———

Contents

Christmas Past

Christmas Present

Christmas Future

Lenten Meditations

Preface

*T*he key to living a life of faith is being continually focused on God. This is not easy to do, because we still want and need to spend time with our families, go to work, clean the house, work in the yard, and cook dinner. The secret to remaining focused is trying to see God in every part of the world around us.

Prepare the Way offers a scripture reading, a meditation, and a prayer for each day in the seasons of anticipation, Advent and Lent. The beginning of Advent may vary by a few days (November 27 to December 2), but the dates of Christmas and Epiphany are fixed. Since the season of Lent is based on the lunar cycle, its dates are extremely variable: the first day of Lent—Ash Wednesday—may fall anywhere between February 6 and March 10, with Easter following six weeks later.

Beginning each day with worship centers our thoughts again on God and restores our balance of priorities and perceptions. Although we are unlikely to stop what we are doing every three hours to sing Gregorian chants, as cloistered monks and nuns do, it is helpful to pause throughout the day and check in with God. We can offer a short prayer, update God on our thoughts and feelings, and devote a little more thought to the morning's meditation.

May your walk with God deepen into a journey of everlasting presence.

Advent Meditations

Introduction

$\mathcal{A}$dvent, the time leading up to Christmas, signals the start of the church year. It begins on the fourth Sunday before Christmas and focuses on the birth of Jesus. The season of Christmas—the time of feasting also known as "Christmastide"—comprises the twelve days from the new feast day of December 25 to the old feast day of January 6, Epiphany. Epiphany, which commemorates the arrival of the Magi in Bethlehem, signals the revelation that Jesus is for all people.

Use the resources provided for each day to help you explore fully the beauty and meaning of the Advent/Christmas season. If you can, reserve the same time each day. Write down whatever thoughts and feelings come to mind for later reflection. End your daily meditation with your own words of prayer, sharing your specific concerns.

The four gospel writers wrote about the birth and life of Jesus in different ways, highlighting those aspects of his beginning that were most important to their communities. Matthew emphasized Jesus' fulfillment of Jewish expectations for the Messiah. Mark told no birth story, his main concern being Jesus' message. Luke wanted to prove that Jesus was also for the Gentiles, and he adjusted the circumstances surrounding the birth accordingly. John, like Mark, presented no narrative of Jesus' birth; rather, he explained the meaning behind the facts of Jesus' life and ministry. Taken alone, each gospel presents a compelling picture of the Savior; taken together, they present a biography that captures the depth, breadth, and beauty of Jesus' walk with God.

Many different cultural and religious celebrations take place in December and January. In Latin America, the festivals include *las Posadas* beginning on December 16, *los Pastores* in early January, and the Three Magi on January 6. *Hanukkah,* the Jewish Festival of Lights, is celebrated in the Hebrew month of *Kislev* (November/December). It recalls when the Temple in Jerusalem was retaken by the Jews and a small amount of holy oil miraculously lasted for eight days. The African American celebration of Kwanzaa begins on December 26; each of the seven days of the celebration emphasizes a different principle of community and honors a specific aspect of African culture.

A $\mathscr{P}$ersonal Journey

(Earliest date for the beginning of Advent)

Waiting

Psalm 27:11–14—David's prayer for help
I will spend this first day on buses, transferring from one to another, waiting at various stops as I slowly make my way across California. The slowness of this mode of travel allows me time to calm the rush of daily life through my head and time to rediscover the difference between "reacting to" and "connecting with."

By taking the bus, I am putting myself at risk: I wait and go according to someone else's schedule; control is out of my hands. The bus tosses me in with people who talk loudly, who eat food of various and conflicting aromas, and whose children are not always considerate. Many different languages sound in my ears; at first, this is a joy, but it becomes wearying as the journey continues. Bus travel is the way of the poor, and it enforces a community atmosphere. The two go together in inextricable ways. Perhaps this is similar to the travel of Joseph and Mary as they went with others, many years ago, to be registered.

It does seem that the more money we have, the more time we spend with the things we buy and the less we spend with other people. Television and cars have moved people off their porches and away from conversations with neighbors. The passengers on the bus will be getting off in different places, but as soon as we get on board our conversations begin.

I am reminded of John Woolman, who in 1765 began to travel on foot to share with other Quakers his conviction that owning slaves was wrong: "By so traveling, I might have a more lively feeling of the conditions of the oppressed slaves, set an example of lowliness before the eyes of their masters, and be more out of the way of temptation to unprofitable converse."

What will happen this year during Advent? What will move me? How can I prepare myself for the unknown? I can't—but I can prepare myself to be open. I can, in a sense, unpack my bags to make room for something new. As I unpack, I also realize that I don't need to carry everything around with me. I begin to see that I don't always need to be in control. I place myself at the mercy of the unexpected, and I must rely on the community of believers in order to cope and survive.

Are the four weeks of Advent enough time to prepare for Christmas? They will certainly not be sufficient if I fill each day with baking, decorating, buying presents, and going to parties. None of these activities goes to the heart of Christmas. Christmas is about a child being born in simple surroundings. Nothing was baked. There were no parties. The only gifts were ones given by strangers that pointed to a future of suffering and death. Happy birthday, indeed! The journey of the Magi may have ended with this birth, but our journeys begin with it.

Often I just need to be in Advent, to soak up its atmosphere. I need to be moved and surprised in simple yet subtle ways. But I have to be patient and wait for Advent to reveal, in its own time, what it will reveal. I cannot force insight to come to me. I have to trust, to be receptive, to seek ways of allowing the possibility of God's movement. This is a time of active waiting, and I do not wait well.

Dear God, sometimes our holidays have been times when more promises were broken than were kept, and they have become something to fear. This is especially true when families are unhappy or parents are absent. This year, help us not to expect specific gifts or events or words that will make everything right, but only to expect you to touch us in some way, at some time, in some place that will let us know that we are safe and loved by you. This is our prayer in a time of so much uncertainty. Amen.

November 28

Truck Stop

Psalm 80:1–7—Israel's prayer for deliverance
Just when I'm full of enthusiasm to do things for God, the Almighty says, "Wait here for awhile. You've got the energy, but what are you going to do?" And I realize that I have no idea where to start. So I wait, although it doesn't console me to read that to God one day is as a thousand. I want to move! I want to get things done! And God says "wait."

I wait at a truck stop, ready to head off in any direction. I've put my affairs in order so that when God finally says it's time to move, nothing will hold me back. I'm all charged up to do loads of heavy work! Then I see God come rolling into the truck stop in an ice cream truck with its music playing, inviting me to take over. I don't understand what God expects me to accomplish by selling ice cream. What good is that?

So I turn God down and continue to wait, listening carefully to God's words. God speaks peace. I watch closely for God's leading. God leaves footprints to show me the way. I continue to wait, with God preparing me until I am ready to move. May I wait with more patience than I have, for the deliverance I seek.

Dear God, may we feel the Spirit behind others' Christmas traditions this year and grow in our faith because of our sharing with one another. May our expectations not prevent us from hearing you or seeing where you are leading, in whatever form you take this year. Amen.

November 29

Watching

Mark 13:32–37—Watchfulness
Traveling and being in new places are activities that lend themselves to watching. Everything is new, different, and exciting. True watching requires me to participate, to be open to the flow of life around me, to be honest with myself about who I am and what I am watching. My

preconceptions cannot protect and should not interpret for me. I am left alone each day to face the wilderness with a directness that takes my breath away. I watch, I react, and (if I am lucky) I change. Whatever I do afterwards, I then do as a different person.

Is there a way to watch? If I watch to collect images, I end up being like a stranger's photo album without the benefit of captions. But if I bring myself to the act of watching, I become part of creation. Sparks of spirit are exchanged. In the details I see the specific. Along their edges I glimpse infinity.

At first when I begin to watch, I see nothing out of the ordinary. I find I need to focus, to put distractions aside and achieve what Whitman suggested: to reset my life to such a basic level that even water makes me tipsy. I need to realize when something enhances and deepens an experience or when it takes over and distracts from or even becomes the experience. Am I eating or reading or sleeping to enhance reality or to hide from it?

I look through eyes that seek out meaning in what I see. But in order to see something, this notion has to be given up. I have to watch each thing and creature on its own terms—to understand it as separate from myself. As I look for its essence, I begin to understand and learn. Watching requires me first to see the other as separate until its identity, its personality, comes out. Only after days of watching does everything stop being special to me and return to its true, everyday nature. Only then can I begin to find my connections and gather my meanings.

To watch is to take in. But if there is no room in the inn of my heart because I have let others fill all the available spaces, how do I let Christ in? If I am to receive Jesus' birth into my heart, I have to create an open space. I have to let go of the jealousies, angers, and self-centering plans that I hang onto to comfort me. I am not somebody because I have suffered; I am somebody because Jesus loves me. I need to watch and allow room for this love to enter and lead me toward wholeness.

Undoubtedly Advent and Christmas this year will look much as they did last year. We will experience God in all the familiar places. This is good, because something very real and necessary exists here. For some, the season will bring a renewal of the hope and joy that have faded over the past year. For others, it will be a reassurance that everything is in its proper place.

Watching for Santa's arrival on Christmas Eve is regarded as a child's fantasy. Yet some of us find great delight in putting out milk and cookies when we go to bed, just in case he comes. This is akin to setting a place for Elijah at Passover. We hold on to our hopes beyond hope because the belief in a perfect time that is coming is important to our well-being.

The hazard of watching for Christmases past is that we look for what moved us last year or what moved us twenty or thirty years ago. That kind of watching is useless. The way in which God moved us in the past answered the needs we had then. By looking for what was, we miss what is happening now. If we tell our eyes what to see, they will see nothing new; we will fail to notice what is no longer here as well as what is here now. We will remain unchanged, snuggling deeper into comforters of redundancy. Christmas will become a rerun, another late-night showing of *It's a Wonderful Life.*

Even if we do not actually see Jesus being born, or stand watch with Joseph and Mary around the manger, or travel with the Magi as they follow the movement of the star, we still know something of their experiences. We must not cover this over with distractions.

By watching without expectations in natural places like Yosemite, I finally can be surprised. Beauty and awe stop me short and remove from my eyes the opaque filters that tell me there's nothing left to see.

Being fully aware of the moment, God, is what I seek as I hike the Panorama Trail trying to find a pace that allows me to notice the small things alongside the path. As I move among the mountains and waterfalls, I don't want to be so focused on the grand scenes that I miss the intricacies of your creation. I want to see all of nature's details and dimensions and thereby come to understand more of the complete wonder of your being. Help me walk in mindfulness of all the levels of your creation. Amen.

November 30

(Feast of Saint Andrew the apostle; Etty Hillesum, Jewish mystic,
martyred this day at Auschwitz)

Walking

Deuteronomy 10:12–13—God's great requirement
The hardest part of watching is figuring out what to do with what I
have seen. How will I respond? If I have no response, then my watching has been wasted. Have I changed inside and now see things differently? Do I understand a bit more about reality or life or people?
Andrew did something with what he saw. He was the one who declared
to John the Baptist that Jesus was the Lamb of God, the one who intro-
duced his brother Simon to Jesus, and the one who later helped a group
of Greeks meet Jesus. Etty Hillesum held on to her faith in the face of
severe persecution and eventual martyrdom in World War II.

When I am walking through nature headed for some destination, my
watching is not finished. My plans always need to be open to revision.
I am still part of the process. If I remain open, I notice more than I
would expect. I see a squirrel at dawn come out of its home and do its
morning stretches like a cat—first with one forepaw and then with the
other. I watch the water in the river for longer than I need to determine
how fast it is flowing, and I discover a water bug sending out concen-
tric circles across a pool near the bank. By continuing to watch, I discover the details that make life interesting.

Ultimately, I learn only from the questions I ask and the risks I take.
When I ask why life is so hectic, is it a wonder that I find peace in
nature? Every informal talk between people is important because the
unexpected can happen in the sharing of two spirits. This is the stuff of
life.

The walk of Christmas does not end with the holidays, even though
the excitement and celebrations are over. There will be other celebrations as the walk continues throughout the year. The cold, dreary days
of January and February are not days for mourning what is over; they
are days of reveling in the change of the seasons—the movement from
preparation to birth, maturity, death, and on to preparation again.

They are days of challenge, of seeing how we can connect the Christmas message with what is going on in Bosnia, Somalia, China, Central America, and in our own neighborhoods. The challenge they present is witnessing, like Andrew, to what we have seen, even though our witness may cost us our lives, as it did Etty's.

Walk the trail. Interact with what you see. Now and then take a side path that is partially covered over, just to see where it goes and to stir up your imagination. See what new feelings arise as you come across the unexpected, the unplanned, and the uncontrolled.

The work of Christmas only begins with Christmas. The messages of hope, love, and joy become our companions as we walk if we are open and share ourselves as we go. Learn to converse well with them.

Healing God, do we believe in your miracles of recovery? Do we trust in your ability to do anything that needs to be done? We feel your presence beside us, sensing that part of heaven is here with us now. We believe that all things are possible if we are willing to let go of our resentments and give of what we have. Let us spend time in your presence, remembering today two of your people, Etty and Andrew. Amen.

$\mathcal{T}$he Gospel Accounts

Jesus' Beginnings

Matthew 1:1–17—The genealogy
Matthew traces Jesus' very human, but important, Jewish lineage from Abraham through David to Joseph. This genealogy bears witness to the fact that greatness often comes out of the ordinary, for it includes adulterers, murderers, prostitutes, and cheats. Joseph is named as Mary's husband, not as Jesus' father. In effect, Joseph adopted Jesus, and under Jewish law, this was sufficient to include Jesus in Joseph's royal line and thus fulfill God's promise to send a ruler.

Sometimes I get caught up in the factual history of Jesus' birth—that Jesus wasn't physically Joseph's offspring—and I miss the point of the narrative, that Jesus was fully human. I think that's all that's being said by the story, a story that seems incomplete to modern eyes because we see history as a collection of facts rather than as a narrative of meaning.

Recent studies on genetics make me think of our ancestry and how much cause and effect are stored in our bodies genetically and behaviorally. If my mother looked like this, I can expect my appearance in twenty years to be similar. If my father tended to handle a situation in a certain way, I will probably react in much the same way. How much control do we have over our actions? Do heredity and our childhood environment determine everything? We are neither controlled by them nor completely free of their influences. Part of who we are is where we came from: our family traits, our past. Our ancestors are still with us. Some scientists say that our brains store the memories of all our ancestors. We are still connected to the past, and this brings us strengths as well as weaknesses.

A minor point to Jesus' story is that even from humble beginnings, given ordinary but decent parents and life in a small backwater town, great people do emerge. Greatness is not hereditary, but the quiet strength of decency can be passed on to one's children, natural and adopted alike.

Dear God of grand entrances, how wild and unpredictable are your ways! Your Child is a scandal from the start, born to a woman whose husband claims no responsibility for the baby. Give us eyes to see and ears to hear Jesus' coming today in ways and places surprising, even shocking to our sensibilities. Amen.

December 2

(Martrydom of four churchwomen in El Salvador for ministering to those caught up in war's destruction, 1980)

Jewish Expectations

Matthew 3:7-9—John the Baptist's ministry
In Matthew's Gospel, Jesus is born as the completion of Judaism. He is the Messiah the Jews had been awaiting for so long. He is the completion of the prophecies of the Old Testament and the embodiment of a new testament. This testament speaks of moving beyond the strict observance of Mosaic law—which had become a listless, judgmental faith—to a faith based on the Holy Spirit.

This was the stumbling block of the Pharisees, the "religiously correct," who were convinced that by perfect observation of all religious laws, they would attain salvation and be guaranteed a place in heaven. Every weekend they would go off on some kind of retreat in an attempt to improve their observance of the religious laws. John the Baptist plainly understood their error. When he saw many Pharisees and Sadducees coming for baptism because it was the current religious thing to do, he said, "You brood of vipers! Who warned you to flee from the wrath to come? Bear fruit worthy of repentance!"

Jesus' new commandment would say that we must love rather than judge one another, as God loves us. The four religious women killed on this day in 1980 were following this commandment. They did not judge the poor to be more worthy of their attention or the military to be more needy of their love. They went to whomever was in need and gave to them what they could. The powers that be were so threatened by Jesus' revolutionary love that they sought to get rid of the women. But this kind of love cannot be controlled.

According to Matthew's account, Joseph is living in Bethlehem when Mary becomes pregnant. It is Joseph who has the dream. There are Magi but no census and no shepherds. After Jesus' birth, the family flees to Egypt. When they return, they settle in Nazareth.

God of our ancestors, we know that we don't come to faith by ourselves. Our parents teach us how to speak with you and how to care for others. Through the example of their lives, they show us how to live. The struggles of their parents and of their parents' parents witness to an ongoing faith that has endured through times that seemed hopeless. Thank you for seeing them through. Thank you for those who risk death to comfort people who may not even look to you for help. And thank you for assuring us that as long as we are steadfast in our compassion and daring in our witness, we will find you beside us. Amen.

December 3

Boom! The Word

Mark 1:14–15—The beginning of Jesus' ministry
Of all the Gospel accounts of Jesus' birth, I like Mark's best—he doesn't give one! This keeps us from getting caught up in theological wranglings over how Jesus came to be here in an effort to prove he's really God and that we really have to listen to what he said. Mark just gets to it—*boom!* The Gospel begins with John the Baptist out in the wilderness eating bugs. *Boom!*—a mere nine verses into the very first chapter,

Jesus appears, is baptized by John, and God says, "This is my guy, so listen to him." And then we're off on a three-year flurry of ministry, teaching, and healing. Healing—why don't Christians heal today? But that's a topic for another day.

I like Mark's approach because it gets right in your face and asks you point-blank, "Are you going to live like a Christian or not?" *Boom!* "Are you going to start being faithful to all the Christian morals, ethics, challenges, sorrows, and so on, that Jesus demanded—with all the rights and responsibilities that go along with them?" *Boom!* Having faith without doing anything is like spitting in the wind; it's the same with caring.

At the same time, I do appreciate Matthew's effort to tie up the loose ends and make Jesus the fulfillment of Jewish expectations. I like things tied up neatly, although I still can't accept that Jesus is related to King David via Joseph if Joseph had nothing physical to do with Mary's physical pregnancy.

I also like the lyrical storytelling of Luke, who brings people together from around the world to witness the birth—the local peasants in the fields as well as aristocratic college-educated guys from a foreign country. Luke's account blends the mundane and the cosmic.

Xylophones aren't your style, Jesus. At least that's what I was taught: no marimba, no reggae, just pipe organs. But I think you are found wherever bagpipes are played for the spirit of any land. I'll bet you can pound the *timbales* and make them sing. I think you like to dance until dawn. You're okay. Amen.

December 4

(Rainer Maria Rilke born, 1875; Cesar Chavez jailed for twenty days during the lettuce boycott of the 1960s)

Salvation Is Open to Everyone

Luke 2:1–20, 3:23–38
Luke's account begins with the birth of John the Baptist. Later, John (in the place of the spirit of Elijah) will prepare the way for Jesus' ministry.

In this Gospel, Joseph is living in Nazareth and travels to Bethlehem for the census. Mary has the dream. There are shepherds but no Magi, and no one flees to Egypt.

Luke traces Jesus' genealogy all the way back to Adam to show that Jesus' ancestors had faithfully observed the old ways from the very beginning. To Luke, Jesus had come to show that God's love was for all people. They did not have to be Jewish or to follow Jewish laws. Luke will later point out, in the account of Peter and Cornelius (Acts 10), that following the letter of the law isn't enough, for no one is unclean or unworthy of God's love, and any rule that says so is wrong. It will be the Jewish authorities, who are so tied to following the law, that will crucify Jesus.

I confess that I slide easily into being judgmental, into wanting every question in life to have a yes-or-no answer: "This is right and this is wrong." And when a decision affects many people, it's easy to follow the standard of "what's best for the majority of the people." Yet sometimes what benefits the greatest number of people is not the right decision, because it is not just. Such arguments are frequently used to continue discrimination against minority groups. Cheap lettuce, for example, benefits everyone except the migrant workers who pick it; they work long hours for little pay and may not even be able to afford to buy the lettuce. Cesar Chavez struggled long to end that inequality.

To love all with reckless abandon scares me because I don't trust people to share what they don't need, to be courteous on the road or when waiting in line, or to sacrifice their comfort for the benefit of others. Yet such a way of life is our calling and has to begin someplace. For us, it started with a child and spread to Jesus' followers.

Rainer Maria Rilke, in his *Book of Hours*, writes of his passion for God. His prayer-poems speak of a personal closeness, of a yearning for God that echoes the voice of the psalmist and the innocent trust of Mary. I seek this single feeling of certainty in the midst of a life of maybes.

Jesus, you have been with us this year, but have we been with you? Like a pregnant woman, have we carried you around in our daily lives these past nine months, nurturing something within us that will be born this Christmas and turn our world around? How will we give you new flesh and new life this year?

December 5

The Word

John 1:1–18—The eternal Word
Poor John, headstrong along with his brother, and one of the three disciples present at Jesus' revelatory occasions, finally comes to understand Jesus' ministry. In poetic language he describes the profound, underlying truth of Jesus: "In the beginning was the Word, and the Word was with God, and the Word was God." This sheer poetry never fails to move me, and it gives me a new appreciation of how the other Gospels enflesh the nuances of Jesus' life in ways I can understand.

And that's the point of all the Gospels: Jesus was truly born as flesh and blood. He lived among us and was one of us. He hungered and sweated, got weary and caught cold, had high hopes for others that sometimes were dashed. And in the end, he had only his faith in God to hold on to—which is what he began with, which is what we all begin with.

Jesus, there is a mystery about you that we scarcely can understand. Heaven knows there are enough people running around trying to tell us their interpretations of what you would and would not do if you were here today. There are enough powerful people trying to force us to believe in their thinking instead of your wisdom. Although you are a mystery that no one fully understands, we understand enough to know this: your coming brought everlasting joy into the world, and we will not be stopped from sharing this with anyone—ever. Amen.

Community

(Celebration of Saint Nicholas, who died in Turkey, 342 C.E.)

Presents

Psalm 16:5–11—A goodly heritage
Christmas is all about getting presents—right? Even if we make a religious translation here and say that Jesus was God's present to us, all wrapped up nice and pretty in the stable, I think this misses the point. Don't get me wrong: I think it was brave of God to trust us bumbling humans with baby Jesus, and it was noble of God to send the holy Incarnate One in the first place. But I think Christmas is more about the presence of God—in our world and in our lives.

Santa Claus is a common image for Christmas giving today, and it competes with the gift of Jesus to the world. Yet its religious roots in the life of Bishop Nicholas of Myrna, who brought gifts to help those in need, are largely ignored and forgotten. The other gifts we think of in this season were brought by the Magi and were more symbolic than practical. They foretold a future of importance, hardship, and death. Today our gift-giving has devolved into buying gifts for those who will be buying gifts for us.

I'm reminded this Advent of the witness of true believers I have known throughout my life. I remember people who gave from their hearts: people who came home tired from work and then cooked meals for shut-ins, people who changed their clothes and went out to build houses for the poor, people who sat up through the night with those going through a crisis. Sometimes only a nod or a lingering handshake from people who were going through tremendous suffering told me that their faith was real.

This year, as the faithful again gather around to look at the newborn, I feel the new presence of two friends in this cloud of witnesses. I see Giff in his quiet dignity as he struggled with AIDS, his smile and the sparkle in his eyes, the way he just opened up his arms and invited you into his life. I see Tippy, who was always doing little things to help others along—letters, gifts, and words of encouragement—even though her battle against cancer left her weak. Both died recently, and I think that this year, when I look down upon the Christ child, I will see the source of Giff and Tippy's strength.

Holy and everlasting God, how hard it is to wait, especially when those we love are suffering with cancer or AIDS, diabetes or heart disease. How very hard it is to be patient when promises of healing so often fade or when all we can do is be present and hold someone's hand. Keep us from the slow, sad slide into misery and depression. Inspire us to stay strong in faith, always hopeful that your love will conquer all our doubts and vanquish all our fears. Amen.

December 7

The Elderly Gentleman

Isaiah 30:12–14—Rejection of the way
I saw him every year at the Christmas Eve service—a quiet, dignified man in his early seventies—always alone. He always looked sad, even with his brown woolen scarf tucked neatly inside his overcoat and his graying hair trimmed short around his ears. He was familiar enough with the service to get by without help; he stood and sat at the proper times. I could tell that the singing of the carols and hymns brought an endearing happiness to his eyes that only faded with the recessional.

One year, I sat next to him to see if I could talk to him during the passing of the peace. But while he was polite enough, I couldn't get him to talk about himself. I noticed later in the service that he became angry and wouldn't sing certain hymns. After the service, I tried talking to him, but he shied away and hurried out the narthex door, not to be seen for another year. What was it in his manner that said it was okay to be polite but not to be personal?

Two months later, I heard that he had died. The obituary mentioned a longtime partnership with someone else in our church who had died a few years earlier. No one knew much about either person. Possibly no one really asked or offered help during the grieving. How could we help if we didn't know? Why would they share and risk another rejection? What had they learned about church not being a safe place to be oneself, especially at Christmas? We seem to invite people to share themselves with us but only if they don't ask anything of us in return.

God who seeks to heal, it is so hard to risk losing my own level of comfort when helping others, to endanger myself in order to help rescue those who need help. Yet I know that if I do so, I will find a place where fear and violence will not concern me. Surrounded by violence, I will feel only peace. Help, O God, my unbelief. Amen.

December 8

Moments

Psalm 25:9–10—Paths of God
There is probably no Christian to whom God has not given the uplifting experience of genuine Christian community at least once in his or her life. We have all experienced times when we've known we were in the right place and with the right people. We long to make these moments happen more often and seek ways of making this come to be. We struggle to find a balance between our doubting minds and our faith-filled hearts, that we may participate fully in a community and help to deepen its spirituality and witness. In all we do, we search for deeper and more-enduring communal sharing. There will be moments of such sharing today if we seek out opportunities to communicate and let casual conversation deepen. Moments of potential community are all around us—special moments when we feel a sacred touch.

For communal sharing to start and grow, we need to be ready for those moments between events. We need to recognize those pauses in conversation as friends tell us the facts of their lives—pauses when they decide whether or not to take the next step and share their feelings and doubts. We need to be open to hearing without judgment what others are saying. And then we need to share our own lives in a similar way and thus complete the circle of community.

O God, my Light and my Salvation; whom shall I fear?
What can anyone possibly do to take you away from me?

O God, the Stronghold of my life,
allow me refuge in your tent from the storm
that rages about in the dead of night,
from all that might do me harm.
Heal me and guide me.
Set me high upon a rock, that I might see your light! *Selah!*

In the quiet of the dawn, I hear your salvation
beating a little in my heart.
With the stirring of the deer along the edges of the meadow,
I feel your love moving into my hands. *Selah!*

O God, may I always speak of your mercy with my voice,
hike the trails through your mountains
with your beauty guiding my feet!
May I always write with streams of your wilderness
flowing beneath my words,
that I may not lose touch with your vision! *Selah!*

God of all creation, may your love always sparkle
in the depths of my eyes,
and at the corners of my smile,
from the rising of the sun until its going down,
as I wait patiently for you to come in fullness.
Selah! And *Selah!*

Based on Psalm 27

December 9

A Circus

1 Corinthians 4:10—Fools for Christ

Christmas in many ways is like a circus. Think about it—I don't think it's sacrilegious. You have the innkeeper acting as master of ceremonies, trying to coordinate the movements of the parade of people traveling by for the census. As it happens, the innkeeper directs Mary and Joseph to a sideshow because only the headliners get into the center ring. There, amid the various animal acts, Jesus is born.

The Magi show up in their regal, pompous robes, looking splendid. Some people from the inn and a few from the town notice the spotlight in the sky and the procession of grandeur, and they wander over to see what is going on. Then the poor shepherds come bumbling in like clowns, tripping over one another, not knowing where to stand, how to act, or even what to say. They get all frustrated, first trying to fit in and then trying simply not to be noticed. When they see the Magi giving the baby gifts, they do something stupid: digging around in their pockets, they find only a chicken leg left over from dinner, and they place that beside the gold and frankincense. Then they go rushing and stumbling back out into the safe calm of the night, glad that the whole thing is over. Yet they know that somehow it's not really over.

I think that this is what congregations should aspire to become: a circus in which everyone—all the members of our troupe of faith, and who are seen as freaks in the eyes of the world—bring their skills together to create a wonderful performance of Christ's presence. They support one another as they perfect their own acts. They laugh when they fail despite their best efforts. And the whole show they put on together moves the hearts of those who wander over to see what in the world is going on.

Clown of God, do we believe in your miracles of recovery—how you were knocked down by the cannonball in the center ring but then got up, how you blew out the dent in your chest and pretended that it was only a scratch? Or do we think that your miracles were only magic tricks that never can be repeated and that reward our belief

with mockery? Do we believe that through you we are able to overcome all obstacles? We feel your presence beside us, and we sense
that part of heaven is here with us now—that all things are possible. We will gather around you and sit in the sawdust in a side ring,
listening to your wonderful stories of myth and magic, of life
coming out of death, of faith that transforms our witness into acts
that transform the world, and we will find new hope. Amen.

December 10

Community

Isaiah 63:16–64:8—God the Redeemer
Being in community is not a picnic. We are not a gathering of like-
minded individuals but rather of like-convinced people. We all believe
that there is nothing more important than Jesus, and we seek to live
with this belief as the center of our lives. But if we are doing things
right, we will encounter differences of strongly held opinions. We have
different ways of getting things done. If we face up to this, our conflict
will show that we value one another and we recognize that honest dis-
agreement is part of living in community.

However, if we don't reconcile our differences with one another, if
we just let matters slide, our sense of community will dissipate like the
morning mist in the heat of the sun. We will begin to distrust one
another and will end up working on our own projects by ourselves.
Good works will be done, but there will be little transforming spirit
within them. If we say that community isn't all that important, we also
are saying that we know all there is to know about God and we do not
need the insights of others.

Does our life together as a congregation seem to be more upbeat or
grim? More optimistic or pessimistic? Is it more important for us "to
dwell together in unity" (Ps. 133:1) or to take God's way into "the
midst of our enemies" (Martin Luther)? Is the goal of being together in
a congregation to reach a state of blessedness, to develop a community
in which we support one another, or to be of service to the world? Or
is it all of these?

When we face outcomes that don't meet the expectations we have for ourselves, for the congregation, or for life, we sometimes want to give up. It is uncomfortable to continue when we discover that our opinions, values, or lifestyles conflict, or when we interact with the world and realize that it doesn't want to hear the good news we have. These are matters of faith. We share what we have; we listen for God's Spirit talking through others; and we humbly let God sort everything out.

This Christmas, we will have expectations. What must we do to make our dreams come true?

O God of compassion, we have waited so long for your birth. We yearn to shed the night that threatens to overshadow us. We long, with people of all generations, to be sheltered in your presence. We desire to be people of vision and strength, that we may sit down and refuse to be moved by the immoral persuasion of racism, that we may stand up and be heard in the heroic fight against AIDS. O Light of the world, give us the vision to see that your warmth is needed and the strength to carry it to those who are struggling against the hollowing cold of despair. Amen.

December 11

Togetherness

1 Thessalonians 3:12–13—Loving one another
Christianity means community through Jesus Christ and in Jesus Christ. Can a solitary Christian be in community? Can we hole up in our rooms, seldom venturing out, never going to Bible studies or committee meetings during the week, and then come to church on Sunday for an hour expecting to feel like members of a warm and caring community? Even if we pray all the time in our rooms and study the Bible for hours each day, nothing replaces meeting and talking with other people, if only on the phone. We need to share our faith with others if we are to feel connected, and this implies sharing our doubts as well as our convictions.

Have you ever been away from home for a long time and longed for Christian community? What did you miss the most? To some extent, attending worship away from home may connect you to God but not necessarily to Christian communal feeling, unless you openly share yourself with those you meet. Visiting another church in your own denomination can help. Even if you don't know anyone, being part of the larger "family" can get you invited to dinner—especially in smaller denominations like the Moravians, where there is pride in belonging to a specific group.

Being part of a Christian community changes everything, for then every relationship we have is interpreted through our relationship with Christ. We are not our own anymore; we are a part of the body of faith, with ethics and morals and general codes of conduct. We no longer can do just anything we want, because now we care equally for the needs of others.

Disabled God, your love is handicapped by our reluctance to share with people who aren't like us, yet it is enabled when we try, for we are your hands and feet and voice in this world. Were our feeble efforts to follow your way of loving enough to cause you to send your only Child? We confess that too often we decide what people can and cannot do simply by how they look; so we won't ask certain things of them, and in some cases, we don't even talk to them.

Flood us with your compassion so that we may overcome the forces of prejudice within us and see all people as fully human and fully worthy of our attention. Send us enough understanding to find ways of communicating with those of us who find it hard to talk or write in words. Open up a willingness in us to seek out ways of working together so that all of us may equally contribute and be equally challenged, regardless of our ability to see, hear, talk, formulate abstract thoughts, or move about. We remember today those who did great things in spite of their perceived handicaps—people like John Milton, Thomas Edison, Harriet Tubman, Ludwig van Beethoven, Sarah Bernhardt, and Whoopi Goldberg. Help us not listen to those who say we can't do something. With you, God, we can find a way to do anything you want. Amen.

December 12

Illusions

1 Timothy 1:3–7—Unsound doctrine
Disillusionment in a Christian community is not only to be expected, it is to be desired. We have to get rid of our ideals for the church in order to see its reality, in order to see the church as God sees it. By recognizing that our ideals are actually illusions, we realize that we need to talk constantly to God in order to keep our perceptions reality-based. There is a difference between how we think things should be (which God may never have intended) and the reality of how God wants things to be. Even with our feet set firmly on solid ground, we will not do everything right all the time.

We will not see or understand everything that is going on around us. We will not always know people's intentions when they do something that upsets us. Even if we have the same intentions as others, we may have different ways of achieving our common goals and our paths may collide. Sharing our differences in community helps us to understand. Knowing one another's intentions allows us to stay in community. We need to try our best, accept our less-than-perfect efforts to be godly, and trust the Spirit to guide us through what we don't understand.

We have images about the church, about what we think it should be and what it should be doing. Even though our images may be ideals, we expect people to live up to them. We have illusions about our congregation, even our own walk of faith. Sometimes it is hard to live with our imperfections when we sense how good and noble a life of perfect faith could be.

Prepare us to receive the seeds of your Spirit, O God, into the fertile depths of our lives. May we be patient as we grow and learn about how you work in the world. May we share our concerns and listen to the insights of others. May our seeds of faith sprout into dreams and these dreams blossom into actions that inspire those around us. Amen.

$\mathscr{B}$ible People

December 13

Joseph Thinks

Matthew 1:18–19—The engagement
The Scriptures say that Joseph was a righteous man and that he was unwilling to disgrace Mary. He was righteous because he followed the religious laws. Since Mary was pregnant through no action of his own, he didn't want to compromise his reputation by marrying her. Nor did he want to disgrace Mary, still having feelings for her. But where could Mary go? Unmarried pregnant women didn't have any standing in that society. He made a logical decision that would benefit everyone. But he thought too much and didn't listen to his heart. His decision was the wrong one until an angel stopped by and told him to have faith—that the details would work out.

The struggle between head and heart continues today when facts perceived by logic are valued over the wisdom of the heart. In a multicultural society, where one set of rules doesn't work equally well for all, it's easy to cut off the kind of dialogue that will improve a situation. This may result in a legalistic viewpoint that preempts a concern for true justice. When I lead with my head, I get things done; when I lead with my heart, people are touched. When people are suffering, it is more important to do the work of the heart than to build things.

O God, we feel for Joseph and Mary—both caught up in something they couldn't have understood fully, yet wanting to do right by all concerned. Help us trust you when we don't understand what is going on, especially if you seem to be leading us in the most challenging direction. When we are confused in our minds, guide us in listening to our hearts. Amen.

December 14

Joseph's Dream

Matthew 1:20–25—The reconsideration
The angel told Joseph not to be afraid to take Mary as his wife. What did Joseph have to fear? Pregnancy wasn't unusual for engaged couples in their society. Perhaps Joseph's fear was that Mary had been unfaithful, and unless something unforeseen happened to explain it all, he would have to live with this uncertainty the rest of his life if he married her. Mary's fear was that unless something unforeseen happened, Joseph would never fully trust her again. Would he be able to live with this big unknown, much like Huckleberry Finn's uncertainty over whether he was doing the right thing by defying society's rules and freeing Jim? Joseph had to decide if he loved his own righteousness more than he loved Mary, and Mary had to decide if Joseph would stay with her and be a good father.

When we feel betrayed in a relationship, how do we go on? Do we blindly trust again, as people who have no feelings and no rights? Do we put conditions on how much love we will give in order to protect ourselves? Yet when we attach any conditions to our love, we bottle up our feelings and hide parts of ourselves from one another. It is better to trust fully and risk being hurt again. Reconciliation, although it is uncomfortable, can be an ongoing grace.

To believe in things as yet unseen, O God, we ask for dreams to guide us.

Will I feel like Christmas this year, God? Will I want to affirm what is good in the world even in the midst of so much that doesn't seem to be going well? Am I ready to be open to people in a way that allows us to help one another get along? Can I let this Christmas be this Christmas and not some other Christmas from the past, or one that exists only in my dreams? I'm not sure. I feel confused. I don't feel ready. What do I want from this Christmas? What are my expectations? O God, I have so many questions for you today. Settle my mind, that I may listen to my heart. Amen.

December 15

Mary's Song

Luke 1:39–56—Mary visits Elizabeth
God lets the proud be scattered in the thoughts of their heads, where they tend to lose their way. We are often consumed with our own importance, thinking that our thoughts are great ones and that our lives are valuable in themselves. They're generally not. We can be vessels for God's mercy, but we are not that mercy. Even though it is vitally important to be vessels of God's love, few people are consistently willing to let go of their comforts in order to help those in need. When the opportunity arises, what am I willing to give up in order for someone else to be comforted? Like Mary, am I willing to take on a daunting challenge not knowing whether I have the skills or strength to achieve it, yet knowing that my whole life will change and that there will be both great joy and great sorrow?

One of our challenges is to choose ministries that involve our passions in life. Too many people have skills that are called into service because there is an immediate need. But then the skills that draw on their passions in life are set aside. The vision that would come from the involvement of their passions is lost, and the spiritual development they would receive is postponed. Only when we are called to give all of ourselves to a task—to a mission—are we challenged to move beyond ourselves and discover the spirit of life.

O God, sometimes we feel like broken vessels entrusted with a treasure far too valuable for us to carry. Help us be humble enough to realize that we'll need your help along the way. Help us say "yes" to opportunities simply because they excite us with possibilities! Amen.

December 16

John's Seeds

Luke 1:57–80—The birth of John the Baptist
John's mission was to prepare the way for the message to come. He had no seeds to plant, but he knew that first the ground had to be plowed. People had to be readied; they had to acknowledge they had problems in their lives that they were powerless to overcome. They had to repent before they would be ready to receive forgiveness. Jesus would then come and sow the seeds of new life.

Sometimes I get involved in a new program not knowing whether it will succeed, and I understand that measurable results will probably be long in coming. If I'm starting a youth group, for example, I know that there will be years of struggle as the church's current young members get involved. Gradually, young families attracted by the youth ministry will join the church. Their children will become active, and the youth group will blossom. But I won't be around, because I will have been worn out by all the effort required simply to keep the group going. In addition, the skills needed to start a group differ from those required to develop that group's depth, and I may not have such skills.

It is hard to remain faithful over a period of years to a cause that seems only to grind along. My hat is off to Anna and Simeon, holding on to their faith for so long. I admire those who believe beyond logic that dreams can come true—those who believed that one day the Berlin Wall would come down, that South Africa would be free.

Zechariah's song is a good summary of our hope: One day we will be saved from our enemies and from the hand of all who hate us. We will serve God without fear, in holiness and righteousness all our days. We will be called prophets of the Most High, going before Jesus to prepare the way. The dawn coming over the mountaintops will break upon us with joy!

O God, we thank you for the miracle of children, for the gifts they bring to our lives with their laughter and their dancing, their endless curiosity, the life expressed in their singing and in their crying.

Their gifts draw us back to the openness and trust of our early lives, a time of innocence that expresses for us what we cannot find words to say. Amen.

A Young Couple

Luke 2:1–5—Mary and Joseph make their way to Bethlehem
Imagine, if you will, a young couple walking together down a dusty country road. After a few miles, they reach the highway and board the cross-county bus. Their home is in Pine Grove, and they are traveling to the county seat in Jackson to register their names for the census. Because it isn't cost-effective for census takers to go to such an out-of-the-way place, Pine Grove residents have to find their own way in.

The couple can afford bus fare for only half the distance to Jackson, so they plan to hitchhike the last nineteen miles. The cool air of the morning has given way to the overwhelming heat of the Central Valley. The continuing drought has left the air bone dry. The young woman begins to feel ill, so they find a shady spot to rest. She naps a little, murmuring in her sleep as if talking to someone. The young man strokes her hair and worries, about her and about what will come. Their lives had finally seemed to be going well when this happened. They don't understand, and they aren't sure they trust what they feel.

They hitch another ride, which takes them another seven miles up the road, but now they know they won't make it all the way to Jackson tonight. It's getting cold, so they look for a place to sleep. They see a motel not far ahead, but the night manager tells them she has nothing they can afford. Just after they leave, the manager remembers the storage space under the stairs. She runs after them and says, "There are a couple of mattresses in there, and with a little arranging, you could be quite comfortable. Only you have to be very quiet. I could lose my job!"

They thank her, and with a little work, the stairway space holds them both. They settle in for the night, expecting that tomorrow will bring what they are looking for.

O God, why do we expect better for ourselves than what you granted the holy family? Why do we keep on thinking the authorities will do what is right, will look out for all the members of our community who need help and protection? Keep our eyes open, that we may notice who is falling through the cracks. May we trust you to provide for our needs when our helping others leaves us exposed and at risk. Amen.

Christmas Past

Places of Memory

Galatians 6:10—Working for the good of all

Christmas is the one time of year when everyone thinks long and hard about how it was growing up where they did. We tend to remember our first Christmases and measure each subsequent one against them. We remember the great celebrations with gladness and the failed gatherings with a lingering sorrow.

Some of us remember Christmases filled with snow, school holidays spent outdoors on frozen lakes and in woods transformed into white wonderlands. Christmas today without snow still doesn't quite measure up. Some of us remember huge family gatherings with people in every room. Some remember the endless flurry of details with delight; others hated the frantic activity. For some, Christmas was a time of great family tension. Too much drinking and too much unresolved conflict tended to explode in verbal and physical abuse, making Christmas the worst time of the year.

Some remember childhood poverty, when our parents made every effort to provide a festive occasion and sometimes not succeeding. Yet often what they were able to provide was enough—a little something special that set the day off from every other day of the year: a new toy, a favorite dish cooked only for Christmas, putting up decorations as a family, or baking Christmas cookies together.

Whatever we remember, may we be mindful this year of the simple birth at the center of all our celebrations.

I yearn to be poor, God,
so that all I have left
is the beauty of nature around me.
I yearn to let go
of the city's pollution and corruption of values,
to let go of all possessions that demand attention,
to be like the wildflower that finds a home
by the side of a glistening mountain stream.
The way is simple now—
to seek poverty of self,
that I may perceive and receive
life's blessings.

December 19

History

2 Peter 3:8–15a—Time and patience
During the Renaissance, three kinds of celebrations occurred in late December: Roman Catholics celebrated the spiritual; Protestants focused on the rational; and the unchurched were wholly involved in the festive, celebrating the fruits of a good harvest and the pleasures of life. In seventeenth-century England, during Oliver Cromwell's time, Protestants and Catholics were engaged in violent conflict and Calvinists were trying to make faith logical and rid it of emotional excess. The Protestants in power regarded Christmas as superstition.

The cities in America that grew up under British influence retained much of the Puritan disdain for ceremonies and festivals. In Boston, for example, as late as the Civil War Christmas was still not celebrated. It was a time of concern for resolving social ills. It took the immigrants from Germany and from other northern and southern European countries to bring in many of the holiday foods and winter traditions that we look forward to each year. Celebrations from Africa, Asia, and Central and South America add a richness that we would miss.

Today we delight in telling stories about a bearded man who slides down chimneys with gifts and flies off on a sleigh drawn by reindeer. We fervently discuss how to feed the hungry and find shelter for those without homes in this cold season. And we quietly remember a baby born a long time ago. In our minds, there is no conflict between these ideas. In some ways, Christmas has become the time when the hopes of all people unite us in a larger community.

God of celebration, Christmas traditions and carols are so much a part of Christmas that we don't know if we could experience Christmas without them. They are full of wonderful sights, sounds, flavors, and aromas that make our hearts sing and our feet dance with joy! Yet sometimes we are so busy trying to fit them all into our schedules that we forget you. This year, help us not lose sight of your smiling face. Amen.

$\mathscr{C}$hristmas Present

Christmas in Wisconsin

1 Kings 19:11–13—Hearing God

Christmas in Wisconsin never seems real until I take time out from the holiday activities and go outside. There in the snow, in the cold and darkness of the night, I finally feel the presence of silence.

In that stillness it isn't so much a matter of hearing the true meaning of Christmas. It's a matter of letting all the voices and noises of Christmas preparations calm down so that I might hear. As I look up at the stars, I imagine the shepherds seeing angels there and the Magi finding a special star to follow. In the quiet, I listen to the distant sound of cars going by on the interstate, the nearer sounds of frozen trees creaking in the night breeze, the happy chatter of parties going on around the neighborhood, and the Christmas carols being sung by people feeling hopeful about themselves and the world.

I continue to listen, standing in the night long after I have run out of thoughts to ponder, hoping that the quiet will stay with me after I go back inside, connecting me with that time long ago. I try to perceive with a growing sense the fullness of a mystery that only seems to become greater as I understand more. I wait in this silence for the presence that will not leave.

Voice in the stillness, help us find a quiet place today where we can listen, that we may hear; and upon hearing, may believe more deeply; and believing more deeply, may go out in faith to heal and comfort and challenge. But first, O God, help us find a quiet place to listen. Amen.

December 21

Serving and Sharing

1 Corinthians 1:3–9—Thanksgiving for community
Giving gifts is not a simple matter. We can give from our excess, letting go of what we don't need so that others who are in need may benefit. Members of a religious community in Pennsylvania give away everything they haven't used in the last year. Thus, they avoid accumulating possessions and they continue to rely on God for their needs. Such giving requires a purity of vision.

We can give from our comfort and tighten our belts a bit. In this way, we learn that we don't need as much as we think we do. While this may cause us some discomfort, it also frees us of some possessions that require either constant use or maintenance. Such giving may be motivated by guilt.

We can also give from what we need, so that others will not have to suffer. As we do so, we begin to learn things about ourselves, like how lacking even a small item in our everyday routine, maybe our morning coffee, can ruin our entire day. We also learn how just a little suffering can make us resent those around us who are happy, such as seeing a family sitting down to dinner when we are hungry.

How will we give to others this year? How much will we be willing to suffer, and how much will we learn? Will we use our skills creatively? Will we make, build, bake, or write something that will be our gifts? And what kind of gifts are we looking for? Ones that are functional or frivolous? What dreams for the future would we like to be given? Would we rather have a new hope for the coming year or a new pair of shoes?

We are a people of the heart, O Jesus. We try to live our lives guided by your love, seeing with the concern of your eyes and feeling compassion for the wounded of the world through the tender mercies of your heart. Do not allow religion to interfere with our faith. Do not let rules get in the way, telling us whom to care for and whom to ignore. Your love is for all people, and we seek the breadth of your vision. Amen.

December 22

(Winter solstice, longest night of the year in the north)

Solstice

Revelation 10:7—The mystery of God
The winter solstice reminds us of our ancestors in the Northern Hemisphere and how they dealt with shorter days and longer nights, the solitude they felt when the sun rode low on the horizon and cold challenged their survival. It reminds us of our ancestors in the Southern Hemisphere, where the longest day was a cause for celebrating long into the evening. Many cultures have traditions involving light in this season—traditions that remind them to look beyond the end of the year, to remember the good things from the past, and to look forward to a hope-filled future. Hanukkah, Kwanzaa, Diwali, and many Christmas and solstice celebrations regard this season as a time filled with blessings. For some people, it means taking a personal inventory of their lives, reducing their accumulation of unused material goods, and simplifying the activities of their days.

The end of the year is a time of returning to nature, of walking deep into the forest and tapping into primordial roots, of going into the womb of the night and reclaiming elemental feelings, of performing rituals that connect us to nature and to the power that illuminates life. It is to pause and sense again that which exists beyond our senses.

When the year's shadows are heaviest, when feelings of self-doubt and unending death draw near, a child is born who awakens the flame of hope and the springlike drive of faith. Something greater is going on here than mere power or knowledge. God is loosed from the protection of our customary shrines, confronts us directly, and stops us in our tracks. We are invited to approach the heart of mystery, to look deep into it and into ourselves. What we find here we may not be able to voice, for it is too near. But we can try to live the vision that now burns in our hearts.

The solstice signals the fullness of winter. It is a time of resting from the detailed plans that crowd the longer days of summer and of focusing on the smaller matters of each day that have gone too long unnoticed. The longer hours of darkness offer us time to look inward and discover connections between our lives and the myths and traditions that sustained, guided, and ennobled our ancestors.

At the solstice, the Northern Hemisphere turns back toward the sun. The Sierra peaks give little hint that they have noticed this subtle shift, but Half Dome and El Capitan seem to hold the light from the setting sun a bit longer. Part of the valley wall between Glacier Point and Sentinel Rock breaks off, perhaps teetered by the turn, leaving a patch of white granite in the middle of the dark gray that has been aging for centuries. Although the creeks and the Merced River lie quiet as they wind through the snow-blanketed meadows, they, too, realize that the time of dreaming is about to end and the time of new journeys is about to begin. Yet to the water ouzel, who dips and dives and plays in the rapids, every day is a celebration, whether it is snowing or raining or the sun is flooding the valley with gorgeous light and warmth. This is Yosemite, and the path of its mystery leads into the heart of creation.

Gracious God, you have the wisdom to speak to us not in the grand and mighty things of the world that people ooh and aah over, but in the still, small voice that comes to us from the corners of our lives, from the people we usually pass on the street without a glance, and from the twinkle in the eyes of our pets. We ask that you draw close and speak to us today. We are in need of your spirit. We need to hear words of comfort, words of guidance, and words of challenge, because we are not fulfilling our potential and we know it. As the storms of daily living rage and twirl us around, help us pay attention to small things, that we may hear your voice. Amen.

December 23

The Day Seems Long

Luke 2:8–20—The angels and shepherds
Even though this is one of the shortest days of the year, the day seems long. The fading light clings forever on the edge of the sky. I want the darkness. I want Christmas Eve to get here. I want more than just the promise of something better. I need Christ to be born this year, tonight, now! My life isn't going so well. I want deliverance, and soon. I know that the tribes of Israel lived with God's promises for forty years in the desert. I know that Isaiah foretold the coming of the Messiah seven hundred years before Jesus appeared! Who could live with such a promise for that long? I can't wait any longer. Let darkness fall! Let the Christ child be born! Now!

But it will be one more night before the shepherds hear the message and find Mary and Joseph. Why did the angels appear to shepherds? Was it because the shepherds had no vested interest in organized religion and so were free to believe the good news? Does this tell us that those who are not looking for enlightenment are the ones most likely to find and believe it? The Samaritan woman at the well is another example of how someone outside sees religion more clearly.

Meanwhile, the Magi had seen the star and were already on their way from another direction. Things were coming together in the form of a harmonic convergence. Things were heating up! Long-foretold plans were coming to fruition!

But I need the cool of the evening, and I need it now!

Zenlike, I wait for you, God, for your words or your presence, something tangible that I can hang onto to guide me. A koan would be helpful, even if I don't understand what it means. In the growing solitude of this evening, as the sunset's colors deepen into their darker hues, the Merced River flows by as a black liquid even though I know it is clear, challenging me to understand. (Does the river only seem clear during the day because of the light?) The Merced gurgles at its edges with a variety of sounds. I try to let go of my thoughts and desires and listen only for you, for what you have wanted to tell me and I have been too busy to hear. So I wait in this solitude, not wanting to leave before I hear a word or see a sign, knowing that opportunities like this do not come often. I know, too, that if I leave too soon, I may not try to listen again for a long time. Through the night I sit by the River of Mercy, waiting for enlightenment.

December 24

This Evening

Luke 1:26–38—Mary's ministry
We are the means of ministry in the world—God's womb, if you will. We are the bearers of God's message. We have explored the dimensions of our longing for four weeks, and now it is time to let things begin. Now we will see needs and try to respond, perhaps tentatively at first and unsure if what we are doing is correct. This is part of developing community. Now we will share our needs and ask one another for help, perhaps feeling awkward and vulnerable. This is part of developing togetherness. Now we will seek ways of working together to fulfill God's love on earth, although we may know little more about where we are going than simply our next step. We will take our skills and talents, our brushes and paints, and trust God's Spirit to lead us into creating art with the work of our lives. This is part of developing our ministries.

This evening we will make our final preparations for the birth of Jesus. We will gather together as Christians from around the world to huddle near a tiny child. We will share stories of the journeys that have brought us this far and pause to wonder where our journeys will take us next. Some of us will band together and travel in the same direction for a while. Others we will meet up with later on. Some we will never see again. But we will remember this night—this one and the one long ago. Tonight we will offer ourselves and our lives to Jesus as gifts for him to use as he sees fit. Although we may not know where we will be headed in the morning, we know that the journey has begun again, with this gathering, on this night, in a little town called Bethlehem.

Christmas Eve Vigil

Isaiah 9:2–7—The people who walked without light; Psalm 96—O sing to God a new song; Titus 2:11–14—The grace of God has appeared for the salvation; Luke 2:1–20—The birth according to Luke

> While they were there, the time came for her to deliver her child. And she gave birth to her firstborn son and wrapped him in bands of cloth, and laid him in a manger, because there was no place for them in the inn.
>
> *Luke 2:6–7*

It is scary, dear God, to walk outside our comfortable homes and start talking about the hope we have gained from Jesus' birth. It takes courage to enter a conflict and say that everything can be worked out if both sides will sit down and listen to each other. It takes initiative to contact our elected officials and let them know that we expect them to do what is just and not merely what is financially and politically prudent. From the unexpected and often overlooked corners of our society come people who carry the message of hope. May we join with them as bearers of the light. Amen.

December 25

(Christmas Day, beginning of Christmastide and the twelve days of Christmas)

Christmas Morning

Isaiah 62:6–7, 10–12—Watchers upon the wall; Psalm 97—God reigns, let the earth rejoice; Titus 3:4–7—All things are changed with Jesus' appearance; Luke 2:8–20—Luke's shepherds and angels

> But the angel said to them, "Do not be afraid, for see—I am bringing you good news of great joy for all the people: to you is born this day in the city of David a Savior, who is the Messiah."
>
> *Luke 2:10–11*

For me, Christmas morning is best spent watching a sunrise while standing outside in the snow. It is waiting for the unknown; it is expecting something to happen. In the minds of those who lived long ago in northern climates, it was a great relief when the sun finally reappeared, unconquered by the night and its demons.

The predawn light gathers my emotions from all the places where they have drifted during the night. I remember last Christmas morning, when I was outside relishing the crispness of the air and staying as far away from the nice, but formal, church services as I could. When the rays of the sun still hidden below the horizon hit the clouds in the upper atmosphere and set them glowing, my heartbeat quickened. Gradually the light crept up through the layers of clouds in the sky and reached down to touch the treetops above me. Then the sun was up, lighting and warming my face. Its brightness increased until I had to look away.

A new day has begun. A new year is about to start. What will they bring? What will be my part in them? Will I be able to hold on to this very human Jesus or gradually lose him for another year to the sentimentalists who keep their divine, ceramic Jesus on the mantel? I want my Jesus to be human! I want my Jesus to be real! That's why we have this birth! That's . . . that's enough thinking. I have to go outside now and celebrate the glory of God's human's birth.

Panhandling Jesus, who sits on the sidewalk in a dark stocking cap, beard, and tattered clothes smelling none too fresh, you extend an open hand to us. Are you asking us for spare change or offering us something? Is it an invitation to sit beside you for a while and rest from a daily pace that leaves us exhausted and breathless? Are you offering us a chance to share stories, to exchange experiences, to learn, and to find a moment of companionship? Maybe you are simply asking us for what we are willing to share with a stranger sitting on the street. Maybe you are asking us to live the truth in our lives. Maybe you are just asking for money. Is that really you, Jesus, hiding in those clothes? Is that you looking up at us from behind those eyes, asking us to share some Christmas cheer?

Evening devotions: Isaiah 52:7–10—How beautiful upon the mountains; Psalm 98—O sing a new song to God; Hebrews 1:1–12—Jesus is greater than the prophets and angels; John 1:1–14—In the beginning was the Word

December 26

(Celebration of Saint Stephen, the first Christian martyr;
first day of Kwanzaa; Boxing Day)

Special Observances

Acts 6–7—Stephen's witness
The Feast of Stephen was once an important religious holiday. The day after the birth of Jesus was chosen to honor Stephen because he was the first Christian martyr (Acts 6–7). Moved by his faith, Stephen stood up in public and preached of the glory of Jesus' birth and the miracle of new life available to all. For his witness, he was stoned to death. A Czechoslovakian carol tells of the legendary deed of kindness performed on this day by King Wenceslas, who stopped to help a person in need. We remember Stephen, who stood up and was counted. We remember Wenceslas, who risked his life to help someone. Both witnessed to their faith heedless of what could happen to them.

Kwanzaa celebrates, over a period of seven days (December 26 through January 1), the African past and American present of African Americans. It is a time for families to discover and enjoy African-style clothes, food, and music. *Kwanzaa* is Swahili for the "first fruits" of the harvest. Each day a different principle of community is discussed. The seven principles are: being in community together, being oneself, working together, sharing resources, having goals, using creativity, and having faith.

Boxing Day started with the tradition of placing a box for contributions in the church after the Christmas Day services. On December 26, the money so gathered was distributed to the poor as a token of the season of giving.

All of these celebrations speak of witnessing to the faith we feel and of being part of a faith community that looks out for those in need. These three traditions merge the inward journey of discovery with the outward journey of ministry.

Spirit of the native roundhouse, all is quiet now. Your worshipers have left. The prayers are over; the dancing is done. The fever of the drums and the heat of the flames have cooled. Only wisps of burnt sage remain in the air. Yet your spirit is still here—in the incense cedar of the roof, in the oak posts and stones that make up the walls, and in the earth which held the sacred fire. Chants still echo here with visions of promise, of guidance, and of challenge.

O Spirit in all nature, may our worship of you not end with the service. May we continue to see you throughout the day as we walk through the forests and kneel by your streams for a drink of water. Amen.

December 27

Solitude

1 Thessalonians 5:16–24—Soundness of spirit
In the winter 1996 issue of the *Yosemite Journal,* Howard Weamer writes about the Ostrander Hut. The hut is ten miles out in the back-country and in winter is accessible only to cross-country skiers. Weamer was its caretaker/host for a good many years. He writes of the wide-ranging discussions that would go on into the night between people of different backgrounds. He also writes of the need for solitude, explaining that "those who welcome it are assumed to have attained something special."

This phrase stays with me. Does being comfortable with solitude mean that one has arrived at the goal of attaining solitude? Is there nothing more that happens once we have arrived? What about self-exploration? Does this happen only in solitude or does it lead deeper into solitude? Being able to be alone with oneself shows an acceptance of solitude. But it is also in solitude that we sort things out; drop useless habits, conceptions, and traditions; and become more focused on life and where we want to go. Certainly solitude is good for restoring our sense of balance, but it can also be transforming. Attaining solitude means slowing down enough not only to see the trees shimmering in the afternoon sunlight but to see them differently.

It is not easy to get people to sit still and listen to the world around them while in solitude. When we listen to the silence of the trees, are we listening with them in the silence as they commune with nature? Or are we listening to their sounds in the silence, hoping to reach the place where we can finally hear them? Every time the breeze picks up, the sugar pines hum.

Being able to appreciate solitude says in great measure that we have arrived, although we may not realize how deep this appreciation goes. So, if we appreciate solitude, I think we already have it and have begun the journey to go even deeper.

As caretaker of the hut, Weamer found he often had to answer the same questions for each group that came in, and he tried, like the Buddhist's bell, to speak as clearly on the fiftieth ring as on the first. He discovered his impatience and, in solitude, learned to let go of his pride.

Today I walk on the trail going along Tenaya Creek to one of the spots of solitude I enjoyed last year. The water in the river is low. I wanted to be here early on Sunday—away from all the bustle of people and activities—and spend some time in quiet, letting a sense of balance and vision return. But it's already midday. It's warm, and the water isn't reflecting anything. I move on and trust the Spirit to lead me to another quiet place.

O God, the good news begins afresh every morning. Inspire us to go forth boldly and with excitement, leaving fear and uncertainty behind as we hike the trail set before us, serving you in holiness and righteousness all the length of our days and far into the depths of our nights. Amen.

December 28

(Murder of the Innocents)

Holy Innocents

Matthew 2:16—The Powerless
During a systematic search of two villages in El Salvador carried out by security forces of the government, dozens of young people were abducted and taken away. Two days later all of their bodies were found, bearing the marks of torture.

After Joseph, Mary, and Jesus fled the country, Herod killed a number of innocent children. It seems that whenever any government feels threatened, it is the innocent who suffer—those who cannot protect themselves: the powerless and the poor, the faceless, those who spend all their time simply trying to survive. These are the ones who disappear. They have no time to lobby for favors. Meanwhile, the group that is threatening the government usually remains safe and generally (and knowingly) allows the innocent to suffer.

With Rome acting in this overbearing way against the people of Galilee, is it any wonder that years later we would hear of rebellious activity against the occupying forces in Galilee? This rebellion heightened the pressures on local civil authorities to keep matters under control, leading them to crucify all potential rebel leaders, including Jesus. So Jesus' birth is not just a happy event. It changed everything—for the better if we believe this birth brings new hope into the world and for the worse if we do not.

We remember today some of the innocents who have been killed in recent history by those who sought to protect their power. We recall Sand Creek, Colorado, where 450 unarmed Cheyenne women, men, and children were killed in 1864. We recall Guernica, Spain, which became in 1937 the first urban civilian community to endure mass bombing by military aircraft. We cannot forget Auschwitz and the other extermination camps, where between 1938 and 1944 the Nazis killed Jews, homosexuals, gypsies, and the mentally ill. We remember the nuclear bombing of Hiroshima and Nagasaki in 1945, the devastation of Rwanda in 1994, and the war and ethnic cleansings in Bosnia in 1998.

O God, protect those who are simply trying to survive and who get caught up in matters of state, pushed around by governmental boards and departments, and told what to believe by those who are guided by money, power, and prestige. Give these innocents the vision to see clearly and the strength to endure until the time when your mercy becomes known. Amen.

December 29

Dawn in Yosemite

Isaiah 35:1–10—The wilderness shall rejoice
I rise in the morning shortly after five, quietly pull on my clothes, and slip out for a walk. It feels good to wake up before dawn, when the stars still shine vibrantly in the dark night sky. Today it's cool and crisp and very quiet. As I walk in the gathering light, I pause on the footpath crossing the Merced River to read a few words from the journal of Brother Roger of Taizé. His words help center me: "The full moon bathes the valley with peaceful light. In recent nights, when everyone is asleep, I have gone walking on the path leading to the hermitages. . . . In a century's time others will make similar walks in the night. Will the same searching lie in them?"

Along the river, the ground plants are dusted white, and the head of each brown stalk of grass is adorned with frost. A light snow has powdered the gray of the valley walls, and there are wisps of frost floating about on the air between them. The light colors of the meadows contrast strikingly against the dark green of the pines that stand silent and strong amid the deep blue of the rising dawn.

For half an hour I suspend whatever disbelief, whatever problems, I have, and I let myself be surrounded by God's love. It is the time of day when God's realm, with all of its promise, seems most possible. For the rest of the day, I will try to hold this presence close to me as I encounter the world in its uncertainty. When the path brings me back to camp, I am ready to begin the day with a spirit of belief.

Redeemer of the sad, the lonely, the pitiful, it is so easy to fall back into old habits, stale ways of thinking that pull our priorities away from you, modes of behavior that don't agree with what we say we believe. Help us be mindful of you throughout this day, that we may hear your directions and escape our old ways of doubt and despair. Amen.

December 30

Refugees

Matthew 2:13–15—The holy family's flight to Egypt
There always will be danger when we challenge the authorities, even if we are doing God's work. In fact, if we are going to bear witness to God's mercy in this world, we will suffer, for God's way of loving runs counter to the world's ways of power and force. If we interfere with business as usual, the government will make laws against us. The police will investigate and keep files on us. Friends of the authorities who have power will harass and persecute us. They will break our windows, shoot bullets into our homes, and harass us at all hours of the night. We may have to go into exile in order to stay alive.

It's too bad that we have no account of the holy family's stay in Egypt. I'd like to know what went on. Actually, I'd like to know what went on in Jesus' life between his birth and his reemergence in the Gospel accounts at age thirty. While the family probably stayed with Jewish relatives in Egypt, was any thought given to creating a new kind of community, as Abraham and Sarah did during their time as refugees? Remaining faithful to God as they moved from place to place in search of a new home, Sarah and Abraham left behind a generation of faith, which would become a nation. In a similar way, we are called to be refugees in life. When we sign on as Christians, we agree to go wherever God sends us—sometimes on short notice, sometimes because of persecution—trusting that all will turn out okay.

Lift up our hearts, O God, when life's pressures weigh heavily upon us. Keep our resolve firm, that we may smile with joy even when everything and everyone seem to be against us. May we build an altar to you within our hearts so that wherever we roam, you will always be with us. Amen.

December 31

Mystery

Jeremiah 33:15—A righteous branch will spring up
The mystery of God-become-human is a difficult concept to handle, perhaps too large for our minds to grasp. Over the years, humanity has gotten used to the story of Jesus' birth, acknowledging that God did do such a thing at one time in the past in Palestine. Of course, there are lots of stories about gods taking on human form throughout ancient-history texts, but we don't tell our kids bedtime stories about them— most of us don't, anyway. Xerxes was such a stitch!

We probably have lost our sense of the immense improbability or impossibility of such a birth occurring, and our sense of incredulity and impropriety that God would want it to happen. We are moved by Mary's bravery in going along with God's scheme (or her foolishness in trusting this angel thing), risking social disdain, permanent exile, or death. She may have thought it was all a bad dream, the result of eating partially fermented olives. Whatever. In the end, she simply said "yes" to the possibilities, and a mystery was born.

We are encouraged by Joseph's decision of the heart to stand by what he eventually felt was right. And even though one gospel mentions shepherds and angels and another gospel speaks of sages from afar, we know that something of worldly importance has happened, and we know we want to be part of it.

God of free will, when we are challenged and don't know which way to turn or what to do, help us remember Joseph and Mary. Remind us that we don't have to solve our problems alone. We always have you to count on for guidance if we but give you the chance. Help us overcome our skepticism and our philosophical arguments in explaining how this birth—this one-time event—could or could not have happened. May we simply believe and trust in this mystery. Amen.

January 1

The Faithful

Luke 2:21–38—Presentation and naming in the Temple
Eight days after Jesus' birth, his family traveled to Jerusalem for the rites of purification. Jesus was circumcised and named. Simeon and Anna ended their long wait, having been faithful even as they entered the last of their declining years with time running out. They were steadfast in their waiting for the consolation of Israel to come, a promise they could have sensed only partially much earlier.

Jesus' name means "God is salvation," and it fit his life's work. Do our names fit us? Do we keep trying to change our identities to match our names, or do we change our names to align with who we feel we are? Are we truly a "Tanya" or a "Robert"? We can lose sight of being who we are. Usually, we can choose to be called by either our first or our middle name in everyday life, but what if neither sounds like us? How do we live up to a name that is not our own? Revelation 2:17 says it doesn't matter so much because we have a new name, a secret one that is our own and known by God. This name is our covenant to realize our full potential.

God beyond all names, Creator of wind and fire, Power of water and earth, we know that whatever we call you, we can approach you with our true feelings. If we are honest, you will accept us. In those times when we feel we cannot share everything with you, let us just say "God" and welcome you into our lives. Amen.

Christmas Future

Longing to Believe

Psalm 85:8–13—Steadfast faithfulness

Christmas brings to the surface many of the uncertainties we feel throughout the year. We know that we want everyone to dwell together in peace and harmony, but we find so many differences and disagreements when we try to make this happen. We know that we want the world to be a happy place filled with love and glad tidings sounding forth like bells from every street corner, but when we venture forth, we either run smack up against someone's unhappiness or we end up suffering ourselves.

So we look for community and sharing in our congregation to get us through, and this brings us joy. But how do we confront and work out our differences with one another and yet deepen communal goodwill? How do we exist in the world as a people of faith when the world doesn't seem to care?

God has given each of us gifts that we are called to use in a ministry. We are called to be artists with our lives, using our various brushes and paints to create a mural of faith and witness. It is by using the differences in our ministries that we transform our community into one of strength. How will we use our brushes this year? What new aspects of the Spirit will we discover?

We long to believe that the birth we celebrated on December 25 will make a difference. We long to believe that our observance of it this year will change something in our lives or something in the world. At the very least, we want our longing to turn into hope, that we may endure with more strength and with more love until the promised time. In Advent, we had the chance to pause for a time and believe again that somehow all our dreams could come true, that God really did become human, and that the hope that lived as a promise within this baby is still very much alive today.

May we come to see that it is within our struggles that the hope of the Christ child lives.

> I stand before you silently
> surrounded by all the glory of nature,
> which makes my heart leap with delight.
> Yet you do not speak.
> Isn't my longing for you enough
> to break your silence?
> Mutely, with your inspiring trees and streams
> and waterfalls shouting of your greater glory,
> I wait in the depths of the night,
> waiting with the silence of the stars.

January 3

(J. R. R. Tolkien born, 1892)

Hope

2 Samuel 7:8–16—The days long promised are coming

Hope without risk is not hope, which is believing in risky loving, trusting others in the dark, the blind leap, letting God take over.

Dom Helder Camara

One of the terms associated with Christmas is "hope." Hope for what? Mostly our hope is for what God will do for us this year. We hope God will bring us peace. We hope baby Jesus will bring faith to all people. Camara's words speak of another aspect of Christmas hope—of what we hope God will do through us this year.

This is a hope filled with risk, because most of the time we won't know what we're doing, or why, or if we're doing it as well as we can. Probably we will be up to our eyeballs in fear at the time, and hope will be very real. The blind leap of faith is involved here. We hope beyond hope. A scene from an Indiana Jones movie comes to mind. Indiana's father has just been shot and will die unless Indiana can get to the Holy Grail in time. There are a number of challenges in the way. One of them is for Indiana to step out over a chasm thousands of feet deep and yet to believe that somehow he will not fall. He expects to plunge and die. Yet with a great love for his father and a trust in his father's faith that he won't die, he steps out and onto a hidden walkway which takes him to the other side.

Tolkien's *The Hobbit* and *Lord of the Rings* trilogy speak of the noble quest, of fighting against innumerable odds and difficulties, and yet triumphing over all. One's strength of determination, one's belief in hope, can overcome the lack of skills and physical strength. Determination and hope can, in fact, overcome any obstacle if we work together as a community.

Trusting others is hard, especially when we have much to lose. Trusting God to take care of us when we give up what we have for others is even harder. Taking the leap of faith is doing what needs to be done, even though we fear we may not survive. This is our noble quest.

Jesus' coming colors our lives with hope. Jesus' presence soothes the pride in our hearts with peace.

Dear God, we want to do your will. We want to shout the good news from the mountaintops about how glad we are that you are in our lives. But what if someone else actually hears us shouting, someone we don't know, someone who wants to know more? Will we feel ready? And what if someone doesn't like what we're saying and challenges us? Will we be like Stephen and refuse to back down? Will we be like Paul and overwhelm their objections with learned arguments? Will we be like Peter speaking great truths and only later discover their meanings? Will we be like Barnabas, stumbling over ourselves and never quite getting things right, yet living a holy life? Be with us as we seek your way. Give us dreams, like the ones you gave to Martin Luther King Jr. and Simone Weil, dreams to guide us, visions to inspire us, and the strength to continue on our chosen journeys when we find detours on the way. With you by our side, we can climb any mountain and share your message with all who happen to hear.

January 4

Seeing the Way

John 3:3—Seeing God's realm

Each of us believes that faith in Christ has made all the difference in our lives. We have been born again, in religious terms. For some of us, it has been a quick birth. For others, it has taken years of labor and undoubtedly caused much stress to our birth mothers. Our question today is "What do we do now?" How do we live as new beings? How do we express our new perceptions?

We know we have to live out our faith, and we suspect that we have slipped back from our initial fervor. Maybe we feel we've never shifted our car of faith into gear. Or to extend the image a bit further, we have gotten the car moving, but we're still stuck in first gear after all these years.

The problem isn't that we aren't committed. We may be overcommitted and trying to do everything we see that needs to be done. Or it may be that, although we don't want to lead, we haven't perceived God leading us into anything specific—something that calls our skills and creativity into ministry.

The passage from John 3:3 says that we cannot see the realm of God unless we are born a second time—that is, unless we are born spiritually. Once reborn, this seeing is the most important element in our quest. First we must *see*. We have to be able to see God and God's spirit in the world around us. The second element is that we must *do*. We need to express our new life through discovering and developing a passion. This is what Joseph Campbell calls "following our bliss," that spe-

were not ready to receive. I think of the cycle of life and death that is played out before our eyes: of the violent deaths of some animals that others may live, of the gradual loss of Mirror Lake and the transition from oak to pine trees as the valley evolves. I think of the mountains as rock slides chip away at their facades, take out trails, and quickly transform places of beauty like Happy Isles into unsubtle reminders of both nature's power and its powers of resurrection. At one time, Indian Canyon was the route to the top of Yosemite Falls. Now this trail is filled with fallen boulders and closed. Once the Merced River flowed where the current trail from the top of Nevada Fall descends. Someday a second rock slide may shift the river back.

With most of the rim trails now closed for winter and only this hike up the valley wall still open, I'm reminded of the limitations of life. The seasons of our memories have marked our days with disappointments and joys, with the starkness of reality and the exhilaration of unexpected joy. There is no banality or boredom here. The elegy of the life cycle records moments of epiphany equally displayed across miles of sheer granite cliffs and in tiny, measured inches of valley floor. Moments of sublimity within arm's reach are nestled within mountains that rise out of canyons filled with mystery and awe.

Nature's voice is clear to all who come here: Look up and around! Can you not hear the joy in the songs of those who have seen this place, even though they may no longer be around? Do you not see the wonders of new life springing up from the sites of massive destruction? Can you not touch, smell, and hear the thousand miracles that are happening every moment? Make haste to sit still, for even the mountains are moving in their slow cadence of life. Listen to the talking of the trees in the wind. Feel the mountains tremble with the pulse of the leaping waterfalls landing back on earth. Hike every trail you can find and catch a glimpse of how much more there is yet to see!

This vision of life is not reserved for natural places but is all around us wherever we are. Along our common paths we see the revelations of life.

O God, once we set off on your path, we may never be able to go home. Once we stand up for our beliefs, our lives may be changed forever. The former passes away, and the new comes. Yet we know that our journey will take us to marvelous places, places we've only dreamed of, and bring us to a closeness next to you. O God, keep us inspired when our eyes glaze over and we can't see what our next steps will be. Beyond our fatigue and frustration with life, let us see visions of awe and wonder. Amen.

January 6

(Epiphany, Christ to all the world, three Magis, the beginning of the season of Epiphany)

A Place in the Mountains

Matthew 2:1–12—The Magi find their dream
Hurrying along the snowy path on a cold evening, we come upon a valley hidden in the mountains. In the middle of the valley lies an orchard that is, for some unexplained reason, in full bloom; without knowing *how,* we know *why.*

I do not seek the fullness of the light now. The forest with its shadows and mysteries, the dark canyons and caves focus my thoughts. Their protected bowers offer me a home among the homes of the animals, a place for me to sit and simply be. It is enough to see the glow of light along the horizon of the forest and know that the sun one day will return in full glory. Perhaps in one of the caves around me there are charcoal sketches left behind by Paleolithic artists that speak in worshipful tones of the holy, an awareness that brought them their humanity.

In this darkness, I find the wisdom that exists between thought and instinct. In the forgetting of self, I glimpse an opening to the other, an abandonment to the movement of nature's civilization and to the celebrations of the night which are pure. The soul of nature so evident in winter's beauty is a creation of God, an incarnation that each season expresses differently.

In this place of solitude, I reach above my head into the fields of stars, peer below my feet into the universe living in the earth, and look into the eyes of the animals around me to discover their curiosity about life. Winter is not the death and decay of all we hold dear. Although it is a powerful metaphor for the completion of individual life, it also speaks of the transformation of each life. Winter is when the seeds of the next generation are readied.

As we sit around the fire to warm ourselves and share the stories of our great adventures from the year past, we also ponder what might happen in the coming months. We begin to dream as life and death dance in celebration in the shadows cast by the fire behind us.

Let the dawning of the light wait! I will linger in the bounty of this season and revel in all its winter glory. Let us eat and drink of the earth's delights! Let the fiddlers play long into the night, that we may dance and sing of our joy of life! And then later, after the festivities are done, we will stand outside under the moon- and star-lit night and gaze around with unbridled awe. In our seeing may we come to understand, receiving an awareness of what this birth has brought and a vision of what this life will be. And so standing as one with nature, may we become whole.

Sometimes, O God, when there is great opposition to what we are doing, when our beliefs are stretched so far that we can see holes in them, we need to hear outside affirmations that what we are doing is for a just cause, that the journey we have undertaken is right. Keep us strong, O God, as we follow your footsteps through the wilderness, marveling at your wonders and little surprises of life. Be our companion as we make our way along our paths to the long-awaited promised land. Amen.

Lenten Meditations

Introduction

$\mathcal{L}$ent is a season of prayer and renewal. It begins with our confession of sins on Ash Wednesday, moves through six weeks of discipleship training and the traumatic events of Holy Week, then concludes with the celebration of Easter morning.

Find a quiet time each day when you can be alone. Read the Scriptures indicated and reflect on the meditations and prayers in this book. Bring into your reflections what is going on in your life. Look especially at those areas that you don't want Jesus to see. Try to be honest about yourself and your life, uncovering who you are and recovering the power and vision of your dreams. Lent can be a time for learning how to live as a Christian. It can also be a respite from one's ministries before returning to them with fresh legs and a renewed heart.

When you sit quietly each day, you join the communal liturgy of all those who are also praying. Our thoughts and feelings are the responsive readings that God hears. When we end our time of prayer, our benedictions rise as incense to a waiting God.

Each week's readings focus on a different aspect of our lenten journey: time, prayer, places of faith, expectations, community, and the events of Holy Week. Throughout the day, pause to remember what you discovered in your morning devotions, and seek answers for the questions that were raised. Search for the presence of God in the people and the world around you.

$\mathcal{P}$enance

Ash Wednesday Week

Ash Wednesday

Return to Me

Joel 2:1–2, 12–17—Sound the alarm
Ash Wednesday begins a journey of turning back toward God. It is a day when we look at how self-centered our lives have become, when we acknowledge that we have fallen short of God's plans for us and that we often do what we later wish we had not done. It is the day when we call all our angers, hatreds, and jealousies out from their dark corners and embrace them as part of us.

We enter Lent as a season of confession. We allow ashes to be put on our foreheads as a sign of our failures, of our sorrow for what we have wrongly said and done, and of our desire to be forgiven. We affirm our intention to put aside every distraction from our lives so that only God remains. We express our willingness to be known again as "Christian" to those who live and work around us.

The season of Lent is also a season of healing. We open up our lives so that Jesus may look with us into the depths of our souls to see the death growing there. On Ash Wednesday, we accept the full measure of this judgment and allow Jesus to remove our burden of guilt and plant a seed of renewal.

When we confess our sins, we accept God's willingness to forgive our sins. With God's mark upon our heads this day, and upon our hands, lips, and hearts during the rest of the year, we believe again that we can be whole if we but allow God's love to move through us and consume us with love for others. These ashes, which were signs of our sorrow, now become our symbols of hope.

> We mourn, O God, because our lives have turned to ashes. Fires of passion and flames of hatred have devoured our best hopes. Conflicts of race and class, differences of age and sex consume us. We have been a haughty church in the midst of a pompous people. We thought ours was the right religion in a nation that made a religion of rights. We try to ignore the weak and those of faint spirit, and we heap praise upon anyone who can achieve even transient celebrity. By your grace, turn our grief into gladness, our sin into repentance, and our lives into flames of your love in Christ.

Thursday

First There Was John

Mark 1:1–6—I am sending a messenger
Everyone was coming to see John, even the Pharisees. They streamed into the wilderness to see the wild man. They came because everyone else was coming. Most would leave when something was required of them. They would leave when John's road show closed and Jesus refused to perform for them. Did John turn any of the wishy-washy people away, or did he baptize them all and let God be the judge?

John was living like a poor Bedouin, eating and living cheaply, so that he could be completely focused on his task. Is there a spirituality that is available to poor people, like John and Juan Diego of Guadalupe, that is not available to the rich and comfortable? John's ministry offered a change of pace to people used to the opulence of temple services, where priests demanded nothing but money for God's sake and spread lies about those who would not follow their lead.

The messenger would prepare the way for Jesus. John knew that he was not the message. He was not, as we are not, Jesus. We yearn to be like John, who cried out in the wilderness, "Repent of your pride, of caring more about rules than you do about sharing God's love, of caring more about your salvation than about the salvation of others." And if we persist in delivering our message, we may end up as John did. The message is the good news, a revelation that we do not have to defend or prove. We simply have to deliver it. The message will work its own way into people's lives.

> O God, help us be like the real followers of John the Baptist, seeking not comfort but truth. Help us be like the followers of Francis of Assisi, who gathered in poverty and rebuilt the chapel of San Damiano, then renewed the whole church by loving everyone they met. And help us be like the followers of Martin Luther King Jr. and Dorothy Day, who seek peace and justice for all people. Keep us from following the lurchings of the mindless crowds who constantly seek new thrills. Help us follow only you. Guide us in sharing your message with all who will hear. Amen.

Friday

Then Came Jesus

Mark 1:7–13—The Spirit drives Jesus into the wilderness
Where were the people John baptized when Jesus arrived? Had they all wandered back to their former lives? What did they want from John that they didn't want from Jesus? John tried to make the people ready to listen to Jesus, but many would not hear. They did not trust the unknown, free-flowing spirit of Jesus, as John, Mary, and Joseph did.

Scriptures say that Jesus looked up, saw a dove descending, and heard a voice say that he was God's Child. Was this the first time that Jesus had heard from his heavenly Parent? There had probably been idle gossip around town when he was growing up that caused him distress, something about his unusual beginnings. Then the Spirit drove Jesus into the desert so that he could prepare himself for his new life after baptism. Jesus was resetting his life, thinking matters through to their logical conclusions, cinching up his resolve to see his journey through to its end.

We also need to get away from time to time, to let our lives slow down so we can think clearly and understand what we are feeling. We need to go on retreat and listen to the natural world telling us the truth about life. We need to read the Scriptures and search out their meaning for our lives. Now and then, we simply need to stop what we are doing, get our bearings, and set off in the right direction.

O God, we seek to be called your daughters and sons, but not because we are worthy. Often we fall short of even our own expectations. We want to be included in your family, because you are our life. Draw us up onto your lap, and we will be giddy with joy! Amen.

Saturday

Now It's Our Turn

Mark 1:14–15—The time has come; repent
John is arrested, and another person steps up to take his place. That is how it is with movements that last. If the cause is just, people will come. Jesus steps up into John's place and proclaims that the time has come. Everything begins now. It is time to believe. Now.

The journey will not be smooth for those who believe. We will disagree with one another. Reproof is unavoidable in a congregation's life. God has given us minds that discern, although imperfectly. Yet reproving is difficult for most of us to do well. We find it hard to go up to someone in the congregation and say, "I don't agree with what you're doing, with what you're saying. From my perspective . . ." We need to speak up when we don't understand, but we must do so in love, in the spirit of learning how God is moving in others.

People in the congregation are often willing to overlook many issues and circumstances in favor of a cruel tenderness that allows other to struggle alone along the paths they have chosen. But we need to share God's word of correction with them as we understand it, trust God to work in them as God sees fit, allow God to speak and instruct us through their response, and then let the matter go.

Whom do you feel the need to confront in the congregation? What is holding you back?

O God, help us grasp the good news with both hands and give it a big hug—not just acknowledge it with a polite nod of our heads as we pass by in our daily lives. Help us to really believe it. For believing the good news requires us to live it in all its difficult, demanding, and transforming details. Amen.

$\mathcal{T}$ime

First Full Week in Lent

Time

Ephesians 5:15–17—Give thanks at all times
Before people organized their day around clocks and hours, they lived their lives attuned to the rhythms of nature—rising from sleep with the dawn and going to bed at nightfall. Many farmers carefully watched the changes in weather in order to help their crops prosper and themselves survive.

In the Middle Ages, Christian religious life was structured around the church's eight canonical hours of the day. Every three hours, the nuns and monks paused to pray. A "book of hours" was created to encourage the laity to stop what they were doing and remember God. To some, the images and words used in the book carried the meditative rhythm of Gregorian chant and helped them to maintain their focus on faith. By listening for God throughout the day, each moment was held open to the possibility of God's direct touch. In an ongoing conversation with God, the depth and breadth of one's faith was explored and deepened. Secular time became sanctified.

Today monks and nuns still rise before dawn to say the morning office together and sing God's praises. Muslims pray five times a day. In India worshipers gather on the banks of the Ganges at dawn to bathe in the purifying waters. Devout Jews gather in groups for prayer at ten in the morning, in late afternoon, and in the evening.

As strange as it may sound, spend time with time this week. Get up one morning at dawn. Go outside and watch the sun rise and the world wake up. At first, nothing may seem to be happening. But as you sit and simply wait, you discover that everything is in motion and that your activity later in the day will be part of something much larger. As you watch, be mindful of how you are feeling and what thoughts come to mind. Notice if you choose to pack goals into your day so that you have to rush to accomplish all of them. Later in the week, watch the sun set and the colors of nighttime settle over the world.

Humbler of the mighty, so often when we're feeling proud of ourselves we know that humility will soon come. It's not that we are humble people, but that we know you don't want us to be proud people. If we are honest with you and share our doubts and concerns, our joys and our sorrows, we know that you will guide us back toward wholeness. But if we hide our feelings from you, O God, fill us with fear. Amen.

Monday

Communities of Faith

Ecclesiastes 8:6—Every matter has its time
Throughout the centuries and around the world, Christian communities have grown up in response to the need for God's people to gather together for companionship, prayer, study, and worship. While these groups often worship as part of a larger community on Sunday, they also gather together during the week to share the details of their lives.

There is something in us that calls us to live life with others. It is at once a longing and a necessity. To be a person of faith means being in relationship—in communion—with the other people of God. When we come together as believers in Christ, we are a people looking to Jesus for direction and for community, for only in community is our faith given form and vision. In small groups, our faith becomes personal and alive.

In the time following the crucifixion and resurrection, the disciples were in a state of chaos. They didn't know what to do next. The great plans that they had been developing over the previous three years had just been shattered. There were no forms for them to follow, so they adapted what they could from Judaism. The disciples felt called to live as Jesus did, traveling from place to place, sharing the good news with those who had not yet heard it. As the years went by, with large numbers of people expressing faith in Christ and the second coming of Jesus not materializing, these pilgrim communities began to settle down for the long haul.

Close Companion, you are as near to us as we let you be. If we breathe, you breathe with us. If we talk, you listen to our words. If we feel sorrow or pain, you feel their depth. We cannot formulate a thought without you knowing about it. And yet what do we know about you? Can we feel you next to us? Today may we find a quiet place where we can walk with you and listen to you. Amen.

Tuesday

Never Now

Psalm 89:47—Remember how short your time is
Time never seems to be *now*. When we were growing up, we wanted to be older so that we could do what we wanted. When we became adults, we were busy working. When we were older, we longed for the time we had in the past. Today is always taken up with trying to get everything done, and there's not enough time. We feel we are using our time responsibly only if we are constantly doing something. So we rush through life like machines, trying to be as efficient and as effective as possible. We have to reach a point where we say, "I'm not going to live like this anymore. I'm going to move at a pace that allows me to keep God in mind."

When I go on vacation, I leave behind my job, my schedule, and the incessant activities I tend to pack into my days as if they were all-important. When I go camping, I go as a pilgrim entering a sanctuary of God. The guidelines I use to structure my days at home are set aside. I am on God's land and move at nature's pace. Time ceases to be defined by the clock. Here time moves with the sun—its rising and setting, and the changes in weather. I begin to measure the passage of my days not by the hours but by my experiences.

> Renewing God, how tired we are. For so many years we've gone to meetings, taught Sunday school, volunteered for pancake breakfasts and fund-raisers; now we're tired. Let us feel again the renewal of your Spirit at our roots, that this time our whole being may be transformed once more and for all times. Amen.

Wednesday

Columba

Colossians 4:5–6—Make the most of your time with strangers
Saint Columba was born in 521 C.E. in Ireland. In his forty-second year, he made his way, with twelve disciples, across the sea to the island of Iona, off the coast of Scotland, landing on the eve of Pentecost. For the next thirty-four years, the Iona Community was the center of his ministry.

Columba's community was as concerned with the well-being of people's bodies as it was with their souls. For them, there was no area of human activity that was not the concern of the Christian faith. In all they did was an abiding sense of the oneness of all; every moment of the day was a time to be in God's presence, no matter what one was doing. This was the cornerstone of the Celtic church: All of life was holy. Living was a sacrament. To pray was to work; to work was to pray. It was inevitable that so holistic a sense of religion would result in improvements in all areas of life—agriculture, education, building, and art. This integration of the spiritual and the material was the mission of the Iona church.

> God of wisdom, truth, and beauty, through this daily time with you, I find my eyes opened. I see more clearly. I am able to leave my concerns behind to see what concerns you. When I come to you in prayer, I am able to leave my needs in your hands and become your hands in my community. Thank you.

Thursday

A New Journey

Psalm 34:1–3—I will praise God at all times

Lent offers us an excuse to retreat from the world for a time each day: a chance to finally take the time to talk with a stranger and make a new friend; hours to share with someone we thought we knew well and discover a new depth to our relationship; an afternoon to listen to nature moving around, above, and below us. We may hear, as for the first time, the gurgle of the creek, the rush of the wind through the trees, the movement of squirrels in the underbrush, even the air filled not with the sounds of cars and machinery but with a myriad of curiosities and joys. Most importantly, such a respite allows the presence of God to touch us, to draw us closer, and to explore our too often hidden selves. Lent offers us a church-sanctioned excuse for doing nothing but letting a place of sacredness grow in the middle of our busy lives.

Wander off by yourself for a few hours. Head to the ocean, the mountains, the woods, or the valley for a few days. Write down your thoughts as they occur, to ponder later. As you encounter feelings you don't understand, share them with someone else. Listen to God speaking through your companion's responses. Find a quiet place in the midst of each day where you can be aware of the presence of God. Even taking five seconds to be mindful of God in the rush of daily activities can restore perspective to your life. And before the dawn of Easter ends this particular journey, find that place within you where God can speak without shouting and you can listen without wanting to hurry on.

During Lent, we walk alone through the stillness of the woods and along the seashore. In our solitary contemplation of the mystery of God, we discover the community we have with one another. Out of our struggles to deepen a sense of community with those who live in the valley of hatred and despair, we find direction, guidance, and enduring strength for ministry. May our lenten journey be a long and fruitful one!

Pilgrim God, we were called to be your people on this earth, not to set down roots, raise families, or build up fortunes. We were called to be with you and to go wherever you go. Like Sarah and Abraham, may we be willing to leave behind what is familiar and trust that your love will see us through the unknown if we but regard all people as part of your family of faith. Amen.

Friday

In the Depths

Psalm 89:1–4, 19–24—I have found my chosen people
Much of our lives seems taken up with matters that are only marginally related to God. Lent is the chance to reclaim a place of sacredness and make God the center of our lives again. Time, space, relationships, and work become hallowed when we bring God into the details of living, for then wherever we are, there also is God. Sacred moments, holy people, and life-changing events mark the passage of our existence. To be mindful of God each day is to participate in a life of faith.

In the midst of our lives, we walk as pilgrims along Basho's narrow paths in the far provinces of Japan. We contemplate with wonder our place in the world while walking on the streets of our cities. By seeking, we find ways of following in the footsteps of the disciples and we discover places where we can hear Jesus speaking to us through the prayers of our feet.

Sustainer God, sometimes hope is hard to live on, sacrificing what would make our lives easier, trying to transform a world that mostly doesn't want to be transformed, all in expectation of what is to come. Yet we know that if we have faith, that faith is all we really need, and everything else is excess baggage. Help us travel light and remain strong. Amen.

Saturday

Jesus Grows in Wisdom

Luke 2:39–52—In the Temple
Jesus' parents found their twelve-year-old son in the Temple, listening to the teachers and asking them questions. His understanding and his answers amazed all those who saw and heard—except, apparently, his parents. Was he precocious? Somehow he had the right framework for his religious thinking, like Mozart naturally seemed to have a genius for music. It was a framework that allowed Jesus to mature. The Scriptures say he continued to grow in wisdom over the years.

I think Jesus always had a sense of closeness to God. As he matured, this sense deepened until he was conscious of just how direct a connection this was and he could put his relationship with God into words. By the age of thirty, Jesus had found his voice and had begun to share with others.

Our time to be close to God is always now. We do not, on one day, just arrive at God's place fully formed; rather, we step across a thin boundary and simply begin a journey of learning and growing. Gradually we understand more and see more about the new life we've already accepted. And one day we, too, find our voice and begin to speak.

O God, we are grateful that you are not done with us yet, that you continue to work in us, developing our understanding, deepening our wisdom, and expanding our compassion. Thank you, God. May we never think that we understand enough. Amen.

$\mathscr{P}$rayer

Second Full Week in Lent

Meditate by a River

Psalm 1:1–3—Planted by streams of water
I like this imagery of the river a great deal. It suggests that those who make it a priority to seek God's presence throughout the day—whether it be by prayer, the study of scripture, or sharing with other believers—will find the presence that nourishes. So often my prayer time seems dry, more of a habit than an experience, and more of a comfort than any call to action.

Maya Angelou's moving poem "On the Pulse of the Morning" uses the ancient image of the river, the eternal from which all life comes, to encourage us to draw nourishment from it, to overcome our fears, and to blossom with fruit for others.

The river nourishes the tree, and the tree produces fruit. Without the water there would be no tree and no fruit. The river waters the tree so that it will bear fruit, not so that the tree will live to an old age. Often I fall into the trap of thinking that the river of life is only for my benefit. This is not so. I am nourished so that I may be of service to others, so that I may share this life and continue the work of those who have gone before me. As my gifts come to fruition and are used, I am fulfilled.

As we pause by one of your streams to rest, O God, we remember your love for us and your willingness to guide, instruct, and teach us about the ancient ways. Help us take time today to reflect upon your words and wait patiently for your guidance.

Dear God, we are experiencing many things in our lives. We feel struggle and pain in places we did not expect, and challenged in ways that upset our neatly laid-out plans. We come before you now speaking of wounds that have not healed, disagreements that have not been resolved, confusions that have not been explained. We ask you to come near us and speak to us, even if we don't fully understand all that you say. May we now share with you what is in our hearts.

We thank you, God, for the challenges and struggles in our lives. Through what does not come easily we learn about ourselves and about you. What we have heard from you and not understood we will store in our minds until we understand it in our hearts. Amen.

Monday

Receptivity

Romans 12:12—Christian mindfulness

At Sunrise

At sunrise I awake to the gathering of the light, to birds greeting the dawn with their songs, to warmth returning to a new day of possibilities.

Focus

The Vietnamese monk Thich Nhat Hanh suggests that when we are washing the dishes and getting ready to sit down for tea, we stay mindful of doing the dishes. Later, we should be mindful of enjoying the tea instead of thinking of what comes next and thereby miss the peacefulness of drinking tea. If we want to experience life, we need to be fully present in the here-and-now and attentive to what we are doing. We must think about one thing at a time and do one thing at a time. When we pray, we should just pray; we shouldn't be planning out the rest of the day.

Listen

Going to cafés is conducive to writing in ways that drinking coffee at home is not. The movement and variety of people coming in and passing by helps to keep my thoughts moving. The various kinds of free reading material stimulate my imagination and help me to see life from different perspectives. Since the chairs usually aren't comfortable enough to sit on for hours and the coffee gets cold, essentially I have one special hour to focus my mind on writing. I never know what I will write, but invariably I will write something that I want to keep. Perhaps going in with the expectation of writing helps me write; going in with the expectation that the Spirit will guide me helps me be receptive to the Spirit, who is always wanting me to listen.

Words

The words we use in prayer are the rivers that take us to the ocean. Once there, we slip under the surface of the water, leaving our words behind as foam. We go down into the vastness of the ocean, which is beyond words, which is prayer, which is God.

At Sunset

At sunset, as the light disperses and the animals and birds return home to sleep, I give thanks for what the day has been. In the middle of the night, when all is dark and quiet, I go outside and gaze up at the stars, opening my mind to the immensity of the universe. In awe and wonder, I think of how much greater than even all this above me is the reality of God.

Omnipotent God, we know that as long as we share in your strength, we are strong. Without your nurturing love, we would be like the disciples—always falling asleep in Gethsemane instead of standing up for you. Help us move beyond our good intentions and the strength of our wills to let you be born in us and through us. Pair our hearts with your heart, that we might feel with your compassion and care with your love. Amen.

Tuesday

Iona

Isaiah 56:7—A house of prayer
The stone crosses in the ground bear witness to what has gone on since Columba arrived on Iona in 563 C.E. The stone of the ancient cathedral's sanctuary, standing austere and gray, murmurs with the devotion of centuries. Compared to the towering cathedrals of Salisbury and York, Iona is small. Instead of one's thoughts soaring up to dwell on the grandeur of God, one thinks of people and God's presence among them. It is good for me to sit alone in this sanctuary, in quiet reflection, and sound the depths of my spirit as I confront the depths of the witness that has lived here through the ages.

It is humbling to think back to the time of Columba and his monks, when they lived in small huts on this island and went off to share the good news with Scotland. It is moving to remember those who dared to come back from Kells and begin the missionary work again after the destruction wrought by the Norwegian raiders. The ruins of the large, medieval Benedictine abbey are still visible down the road. It is inspiring to imagine the excitement of George MacLeod and the small Iona Community in 1938 as they began their challenging work on Iona to renew the mainland Scottish churches. And it is simply good to be where a friend, John Oliver Nelson, founder of the Kirkridge Retreat Center in Pennsylvania, had his spiritual home. To walk the hills of the island, to sit in the ruins of ancient buildings, to meditate in the small chapel is to feel the presence of all this enduring faith.

As people enter the chapel for worship, the sanctuary begins to hum with faith. People are waiting for the movement of God in this quiet atmosphere; they are open to guidance and inspiration and are attuned to the presence of God in one another. A recorder begins playing and fills the nave with warm sounds. The music brings the echoes of our different paths of faith into unity and common worship.

May I carry the simplicity of Iona's spirit within me wherever I go.

Deep-running is your wisdom, O Fountain of living water, and longer lasting than anything this world can offer. Our concerns fade as new concerns arise. Generations pass. Whole nations give way to others, yet your wisdom remains largely unknown to us. May we learn to listen to the sound of your rushing water, touch its coolness to our troubled foreheads, and carry this water to people instead of carrying our fears and doubts. Amen.

Wednesday

The Night Sky

Psalm 8:3–4—The heavenly bodies

When I look at your heavens, the work of your fingers, the moon and the stars that you have established; what are human beings that you are mindful of them?

Psalm 8:3–4

Looking up in the quiet of a dark night, feeling the warmth of the earth on my back, I become lost in the wonder of the stars. I imagine playing hopscotch with a meteor on an invisible sidewalk that stretches past Jupiter and Saturn and makes a big turn at Pluto, as if I were in God's playground. The elemental nature of the galaxies leaves me in awe. The beginnings of the universe are there, untouched although not unchanged by the passage of time. I am humbled. Compared to the vastness of it all, why should I be of any importance? I'm not, and that's okay. But I am part of everything that is going on, and this makes me larger than myself. As Carl Sagan says, we're made of star stuff, and this thought sends my head spinning off toward the Orion Nebula.

"The work of your fingers," fingers like my own—a human image that would seem to limit the powers of the Creator. But having witnessed humans' ability to create wondrous things with their hands, to build, to comfort, and to heal, my mind explodes with the possibilities of God being behind even a single pair of human hands.

The movement of the moon through the sky marks the orderly passage of time. The Gregorian calendar runs slightly off the lunar cycle and reminds me that our time is not always God's time. This calls me back to seeking God's pace. The moon's effect on the tides suggests how even a little of God's beckoning can move me great distances. The light of the moon, being a reflection of the sun, illustrates that I am to be such and reflect God's light. I am not the source. And like the moon, I, too, have a dark side which few see.

Nighttime on top of Glacier Point scares me, God. There is no railing in front of the three-thousand-foot drop, and I've forgotten where the edge is. Behind me is the untamed wilderness with its very real bears and mountain lions. The last few people have left to go back down to the valley and taken the remaining lights with them. Standing here in the darkness between the stars above and the campfires below, I feel suspended between heaven and earth. If I can wait through my uneasiness, I may learn something. With little to hold on to but the awe that transfixes my imagination, I wait for you to come.

Thursday

Prayer Time

Isaiah 26:1–4—Open the gates
Prayer time is an opportunity to realize what is going on in your life—to sort out goals and tasks and prioritize them. It is a time for discovering the difference between what you want and what you need. And it is a time to share with God—not that God doesn't already know what is going on in your life. God is omniscient. But if you can't verbalize what is going on, then you probably don't know.

The first big step in prayer is to stop talking to God and begin sharing with God. The next step is to listen for God. This requires silence—emptying the mind of your everyday cares. Playing soft music, focusing on a candle, or repeating a set prayer can help. The critical challenge is to move from trying to decide what God wants you to do to letting God direct you through the murmurs you hear during prayer and the ever-so-soft nudges you feel during the day. These are subtle influences, which we perceive only if we are waiting and listening for them.

The life of prayer is a journey with God as well as toward God—a journey in which prayer becomes, for those who faithfully pursue it, as natural and as necessary as breathing. When everything we do is done in prayer, the benefits we reap are an increase in love, patience, and compassion for others, and a lingering touch of holiness.

Womb of God, through you we are born again and have life, and each day is a celebration of the joy of creation and creating. Now alive with your intimate love, we are part of your birthing and rebirthing of this world. May we be midwives in your name. Let us remember today those women of many nations and countless ages who have gone before us: Ruth, Leah, Sarah, Vashti, Esther, Lydia, Hannah, Sojourner, Rosa, Dorothy, and many others. Let us witness with their spirit by rejoicing, praying, and giving thanks in all circumstances. Let us witness by seeking justice and loving mercy. Amen.

Friday

The Prayer of Our Savior

Matthew 6:7–15—Pray from your heart
To be mindful of God throughout the day is a grace and the foundation for living a life of faith. The words of the Prayer of Our Savior offer us a structure for thinking about the dynamics of Christian living. Too often, many of us (having said the prayer so often) simply repeat the words without thinking about them. Take time this season to carefully look at them. Listen to your needs being identified by the prayer's passages. Discover through its guidance the needs of people who live and work around you. Feel words of concern rise from your heart. Share them with others. Uncover your dreams and abilities as you enter ministries never before imagined.

Instead of using the expected tone of "Almighty God, Omniscient Ruler," in this prayer Jesus uses "Father," a familiar image that everyone can relate to directly, one that has a sense of parental closeness rather than of distance, of approachability rather than of judgment, of relationship rather than of power. Jesus' use of the personal "Father" in referring to God—which is more accurately translated as "Daddy"—did not come out of the Jewish tradition. In fact, we find it hard to comfortably use "Daddy" in formal worship settings ourselves, although we might use it in our personal prayer. Jews used the more formal "Father," although sparingly out of respect for the Ruler of the universe. So God as "our Daddy" was a new term, as was Jesus' emphasis on approaching all prayer in this way, for we are in a dependent relationship with God, which we never outgrow.

Give us, dear Parent, what we need for today, not what we want. Do not give us so much that we are tempted to stockpile it for the future; for if we try, it will spoil, like manna. Give us just enough to feed us today so that we may travel light, so that we will continue to need you, to rely on you and not on ourselves. Remind us always that our possessions are not due to anything we've done by ourselves and that persons who have more are no more blessed in your eyes. We thank you that all good things come from you in due season. Amen.

Saturday

The Iona Community

James 2:14–18—Faith and works
The Iona Community is an ecumenical group founded in 1938 by George MacLeod to be "both a cradle and a challenge" for the church in facing the matters of faith in the twentieth century. The community evolved out of MacLeod's eight years as pastor in a poor area of Glasgow, Scotland. That experience convinced him that there was an urgent need for the church to find new ways of meeting the needs of working-class people.

MacLeod felt that to preach of the bread of life to unemployed and despairing people with hungry families, without being actively concerned with their physical needs, was a betrayal of Jesus' message. He thought that the church was unlikely to adapt to the new conditions unless its pastors received different training. So he resigned his parish and set off for the island of Iona with a half-dozen artisans and a half-dozen pastors to start the Iona Community.

On Iona the "priesthood of all believers" was lived out and the cathedral was rebuilt. As more people joined the community, the work shifted to the mainland, where new ministries were developed, especially those dealing with shortages of housing and food. Today Iona also has centers for Christian unity, healing, and youth work.

Architect God, as we forget ourselves, we become part of you and part of one another in your community of faith. As we turn away from what tears down, you bring us the raw materials to build something new. May what we design—whether it be buildings or the building-up of people—be strong, honest, and serviceable to the needs of the world. Amen.

$\mathcal{P}$lace

Third Full Week in Lent

Sunday

Sacred Places

Psalm 29:9—The voice in the oaks

Not only time but place becomes sacred when we carry God with us. There are some places—quite ordinary by themselves—where we simply feel closer to God, where our thoughts settle and we feel the beating of our hearts of faith. A favorite spot on a river or a beach or a familiar path through the woods brings our thoughts back to God. Places like Yosemite Valley, with its granite walls, the savannas of Masai Mara in Kenya, and Yangshuo, China, with its pine trees and mist, inspire us with the majesty of their natural wonder. Sometimes seasons bring people closer to God. Winter snow or rainstorms that make travel difficult foster solitude, encouraging us to stay indoors and invite God to be present.

In places where past civilizations worshiped, we are moved to understand their traditions and to explore the depths of our own spirituality. Where people knelt to pray centuries ago, we feel a special energy—places like Taos Pueblo in New Mexico, Machu Picchu in Peru, Hebron and Mount Sinai in the Middle East. Being in places where God has made special revelations—as in Guadalupe, Mexico; Sounion, Greece; or Lourdes, France—encourages us to believe that we, too, can feel God's presence in life-changing ways.

There are special places where we hear an echo of the immortal, places where our spirits rise like incense, where the inner and outer forces in our lives meet. Such places as France's Chartres Cathedral, the monoliths of Stonehenge, and the buildings of Angkor Wat in Cambodia witness to the need of all people in every time to seek out the sacred, to express their faith through a constructive creativity that inspires others. Even places that exist only in myths and places we've never been are enough to stir up our imaginations and put us in touch with the Spirit.

Sacred places open my everyday world to the dimension of mystery. Yosemite is one such place. All is alive, all changing with the movement of the seasons, all charged with the sacredness of flowers and the grandeur of mountains. Always there is something to remember, something that touches, moves, or surprises me. So I travel to the valley. Sometimes it's good just to be there, without anything being new or spectacular, without there being any one experience I can point to later and say that made it all worth while. Without fail, I come away renewed.

God of many names—God of love and hope and laughter; foolish God who chooses the lowly, the poor, the obscure; Maker of rainbows; Midwife of changes; Breath of life; Earthen vessel—all people are a part of you, no matter by what name they know you. Help us realize that as we draw closer to others, we draw closer to your Spirit and to your truth. Amen.

Monday

The Bohemian Brethren

Ezekiel 11:16–17—A sanctuary for those scattered
In the late fourteenth century, the Reverend Jan Hus began to press for certain reforms in the Catholic church. He wanted services to be held in the peoples' own language so they could understand what was going on. He wanted laypeople to receive wine as well as the bread during communion, because they were also the body of Christ. And he wanted

a return to the Bible as the source of faith. Because Hus threatened the power of the church authorities, they declared him a heretic and burned him at the stake in 1415.

Those who had found a renewal of their faith through Hus's preaching refused to give up his reforms. The church responded by sending in the military. The Hussites responded by taking up arms and pushing the Catholics out of Bohemia and Moravia. In 1457, these followers organized into the first Protestant church, the Bohemian Brethren, sixty years before Martin Luther led the Protestant Reformation in Germany.

The Bohemian church prospered in the sixteenth century, writing hymns, translating the Bible into Czech, building schools, and improving farms, much as had been done on Iona. In the early seventeenth century, the Catholic Counter-Reformation swept the land, forcing Bohemians to become Catholic, die, or go into exile. Early in the 1700s, a small group of these exiles from Moravia gathered in Herrnhut, Germany, and renewed the Bohemian church. Once again the church prospered.

From this small community of 250 in Herrnhut, one hundred missionaries were sent around the world, spurring Baptists in England to start their own mission society. Hymn-writing flourished. A prayer meeting led to a resolve to have someone in prayer at all times, and this lasted for more than a century. A daily devotional premiered in 1731 and continues to be published annually. Dietrich Bonhoeffer drew strength from these daily texts while he was imprisoned during World War II. Communal groups were initiated in European centers to foster ecumenism, and the one in London inspired the Wesleys to begin the Methodist church. Settlements in Pennsylvania and North Carolina brought these German Moravians to North America in the mid-1700s. There they lived communally and, through pacifism, tried to resolve the hostilities between European colonists and the American Indians.

Kind God, we come before you knowing that we have failed in so many ways this week. There have been times when we have drawn back from what was right, because it was difficult. Forgive us for our self-centeredness, our weakness, and our despair. Give us courage to accept healing for our brokenness. Come, Christ Jesus, come. Amen.

Tuesday

Being Aware

Psalm 14:4—Awareness
The powerful who eat up people as easily as they eat bread, who use up people as their right and privilege, are leading a corrupt life. Their corruption rises out of their refusal to seek God and results in violence toward the people of God, who call them to account for their actions, and toward all people under their control. What comes to mind are the banana republics in Central America, the tin mines in Bolivia, the coffee plantations in Colombia, and the prison labor camps in China, where workers live in poverty so that we may have our "necessary" comforts. Those who use products made cheaply by such labor are like those who claim they have no knowledge of the suffering involved. We know—or we should know. We see the "Made in China" label and shrug off whatever reservations we have as "probably not from the labor camps," where political prisoners are routinely tortured and killed.

When does "business as usual" reach a line we ethically dare not cross? When does the drive to maximize profits need to turn back toward a fair return for the workers? Who is guilty? The owners of the operation and the investors, who know how the material is being produced? The ones who buy the cheap products and don't care who suffered to produce them? Those who aren't involved, yet know the truth and still do nothing?

And if those who are exploited choose to stay because they need the job and can't find anything else, is the system then rendered just?

Carpenter of all creation, that to which we devote our time will give evidence of our work. If we work for you part-time, then we won't have much to show you. If we spend our time on matters that we don't value, we can take no pride in our accomplishments. But whatever we do—whether it be carpentry, bathing lepers in Calcutta, farming the land, typing reports, or visiting friends over a cup of tea, let us work hard for you, with honest labor. Amen.

Wednesday

The Taizé Community

Daniel 9:17–18—Shine upon the desolation
Brother Roger first came to the village of Taizé, France, in 1940. He dreamed of starting a community "on account of Christ and the Gospel," and he chose to do so in an area ravaged by World War II. His house became a place of welcome for refugees, especially Jews fleeing the Nazi occupation. After living alone for two years, he was joined by his first brothers, and in 1949, when there were seven of them, they committed to life together.

Taizé's vocation is to strive for communion among all. From its beginning, the community has worked for reconciliation among Christians split apart into different denominations. But the brothers do not view reconciliation among Christians as an end in itself. Reconciliation concerns all humanity, and it makes the church a place of communion for people of all religions and nations.

During the first twenty years of its existence, the community lived in relative isolation. Then gradually young people began coming to Taizé in ever-increasing numbers. Out of this grew the idea of holding a "Council of Youth." Opened at Taizé in 1974 with forty thousand young people, it has involved people from all over the world in an ongoing program of dialogue. Young people from many different countries enter into the prayer of the community and share their lives and concerns with one another; they look for ways that they can live lives of prayer and commitment back home. Others come to Taizé to confront the gospel in the solitude of a silent retreat.

Healer of memories, sometimes I forget that the miracles that transform can be as common as a sunny day, a warm smile, a hug from someone who has angered me, or the joy of making friends with a stranger. Do I need the big miracles of physical healing or the partings of a sea in order to believe? Not as long as I remember your miracle of life itself. Amen.

Thursday

Hard Sayings

John 6:60—Difficult teachings
How are we to read and understand passages in the Scriptures that speak of hatred and violence? It is hard on several levels to like passages such as the following:

"Let their eyes be darkened and make their loins tremble" (Ps. 69:23–28).

"Thou hast broken the teeth of the ungodly" (Ps. 3:7).

"Happy shall he be, that taketh and dasheth thy little ones against the stones" (Ps. 137:9).

"I hate them with perfect hatred" (Ps. 139:22).

"Let burning coals fall upon them" (Ps. 140:10).

It is hard to respect the people of faith who would want such horrible things to be done, hard to trust a God who would actually carry them out, and hard for us to admit that we would wish such events upon another person.

Yet at times we do mutter similar things under our breath. At times we do want God to do truly terrible things to those who seem to deserve such anguish, such pain, and such sublime suffering that they will repent from their evil ways and promise never, ever, to do anything like that again, upon their sainted mothers' heads. We really do like people to get a taste of their own medicine: nice things for the nice people; broken teeth for the nasties.

We can try to soften the harshness by saying it's all part of God's system of justice; we can ask for all the retribution we want, but only God will decide what to do. Then if God decides to poke them in the eye, kick them in the knee, or run their car into a tree . . . well, what control do we have over that? We do feel like this psalmist at times, before our charity takes over. So we shouldn't be shocked when we read such passages. It's real. It's us.

Coyote challenges me, God, playful, yet doing whatever is necessary to survive. Coyote reminds me of you—the loving God of the New Testament, filled with radiance and warmth and beauty. But Coyote also reminds me of the vengeful God of the Old Testament, ready to punish all who do not measure up. I saw this aspect of you around Tioga Pass, in the Bloody Canyon area, where the beauty of Yosemite ends and the fear of chaos begins. What am I to make of you?

Friday

Yosemite Inspiration

Ezekiel 8:1–4—The Spirit lifted me up between heaven and earth
When I need to be inspired to my depths, I head for the heights of Yosemite. My favorite area is high above the valley on the rim trails that run under the shade of the forests. Getting there takes a deliberate effort, usually two to three hours of strenuous hiking. There are only a few people at seven thousand feet. Here it is cool and quiet. I can take off my hat and hold it in my hand without the risk of my face getting sunburned. From many viewpoints, I can see out over the peaks and domes of the Sierra into the mystery of the deeper wilderness and down into the meanderings of the valley a mile below.

Up here I lose sense of where my skin ends and Yosemite begins. When a breeze comes up on a warm day, I find that the forest and I breathe together. When I cross a gurgling creek, I don't hear it with my ears but rather somewhere in the middle of my chest. I'm aware of birds lighting on the branches beside me almost before they do, and I am as aware of the movement of the trees in the breeze above me as I am of my own movement. I see squirrels shuffling in the leaves on the ground behind me, even though I hear but a single sound. I can tell what is around me by the scents, even the time of day, for the sun warms the rocks, trees, bushes, and open ground differently and incrementally. It's not that I feel like one of the creatures of the forest. It's more that all of us are being held up by something greater, that the same creative force that moves in and through everything in Yosemite is also moving through me.

Walking under this shady, forest canopy feels like walking through a cathedral of trees, where Ponderosa pines reach up hundreds of feet, where grace is expressed in things granite and green, and where the stations of the cross appear as boulders left and marks etched into stone by glaciers ten thousand years ago. The sounds of the streams are both offertory and benediction—the unending alleluias and eternal amens flowing over each other effortlessly and endlessly. Steller's jays call all who are willing to come to this table of the wilderness; there they celebrate a subtle mass and distribute acorns to all who will accept them. The water of the creeks is full of the taste of the highlands. This is a place where God's blessing comes down on all creation equally and with so much abundance that it leaves me in a state of euphoria.

We confess, O God of all creation, that we hide behind church forms for assurance when we feel unsure, that too often we let our Sunday worship take the place of our faith. Instead of praying each day on our own, we let the church's Sunday prayers be our prayer for the week. Instead of dealing with the responsibilities that our participation in communion gives us, we let our participation in the service be the extent of our ministry. Instead of leaving here to share the good news with the world, we let our pastors shoulder this responsibility. We have become like hollow buildings, full of strength and beauty but empty inside. Each new problem that drops into our lives echoes with our lack of faith.

Help us, O God, to feel again your movement in our lives. Help us share again with others and see what your hope means to them. Help us be faithful again to a simplicity of living, that nothing may get in the way of serving you. Help us always to love one another, that our differences will not build new walls of separation. Help us celebrate the sacredness of every living thing and the presence of your Spirit in every individual, that we may be a true and enduring community.

The Koinonia Community

Acts 2:44–47, 4:32–35—All who believed held their possessions in common

In 1942, Clarence and Florence Jordan and Mabel and Martin England founded Koinonia Farm near Americus, Georgia. Drawing its name and operating principles from the books of Acts, Koinonia was to be an example of Christian community in which members pooled their resources and shared all things in common. Although they had some agricultural training, none of them had much practical experience. Clarence Jordan, who earned a doctorate in New Testament Greek, had been an inner-city missionary in Louisville, Kentucky. He would write the Cotton Patch Version of the New Testament. England and his wife had served as American Baptist missionaries in Upper Burma.

Working, eating, and living side by side, black and white Koinonians intended to show by example the benefits of reconciliation between the races. Ku Klux Klan members repeatedly visited them to warn against the mixing of the races. In 1950, the Rehobeth Baptist Church voted to withdraw from community with the Koinonians because of differences on "the race question."

Most of the people who came to live at Koinonia had heard Clarence Jordan speak at conferences across the country. By 1956, the population had reached sixty. Then a decade of vandalism, violence, fraudulent tax investigations, and economic boycotts against Koinonia began. Unable to support itself any longer by farming, Koinonia developed a pecan and fruitcake mail-order business which involved minimal local interaction.

In 1965, Linda and Millard Fuller arrived and developed a plan whereby Koinonia would build low-cost houses for people living in substandard dwellings. The Fund for Humanity was set up to provide capital, a fund that would also support the development of other businesses, including sewing and pottery-making. Clarence Jordan died in 1969, but others continued the work. In 1979, the population was back up to thirty-six adults, and Koinonia partners had built 180 houses in the county. In 1976, the Fullers left Koinonia to establish Habitat for

Humanity International. In 1979, three couples left to form Jubilee Partners, a sister community in northern Georgia which works with refugees coming into the United States.

Farming today at Koinonia is organic, seeks to be ecologically responsible, and employs fifty local residents. The watchwords for Koinonia, Christian pacifism, racial reconciliation, and simple living, continue to guide their ministry.

God of wounded hands, you came into the world not to be king, as many thought, but to be a servant. You came not to sit at the right hand of God, but to live by the side of the road and tend to the needs of people passing by. May our hands be worn down by endless toil for those who need help and those who are persecuted. May our hands be broken by the butts of guns if that is what's needed to heal in your name. Amen.

$\mathcal{E}$xpectations

Fourth Full Week in Lent

Traditions

2 Thessalonians 2:15—Hold fast to tradition
When we pray or try to get close to God, we call on what we have been taught: the traditions of our faith, the devotional style of our denomination, the particular religious nuances of our family. We were taught to talk to God in a certain way, shown that we can only approach God on bended knee, told that there is a specific way to ask things of God and a specific time when it is proper to ask. Yet what we have been taught sometimes gets in the way of our prayer because it isn't always consistent with who we are or how we have experienced God.

Even our own memories of how we have known God in the past can prevent us from knowing God now. Once, for example, when I was thinking about other matters, I felt the presence of God near a river. Now every time I'm near that river, I partially expect to experience God again in that same way. I haven't experienced God's presence there since that time; sometimes I even fail to notice how the river is now because I close myself off to really seeing it.

Observing how other faiths draw close to the sacred can help us break through the roadblocks in our tradition's old forms. For example, hearing the Prayer of Our Savior spoken in different words allows us to move beyond the repetition of the familiar words to focus on the meaning of the new words. It is important to use the traditions that help us in our lives of faith and to set aside the ones that do not. Traditions should lay a foundation on solid ground and inspire us to use our imagination to build upon it with the raw material of our experiences. We use traditions too often to try to tame God's wildness, to keep God in a cage like an animal whose spirit is gradually broken. It is as if we say, "We have all of God's essence preserved for all time. Want to see?" But God cannot be contained, and God refuses to be tamed. So when we pray, we need to pray as who we are, and allow God the flexibility to be God.

God of Jewish faith, why do tragedies happen to faithful people? Why do people disagree about what you want? Why do those who leave all behind to serve you seem to suffer more? Why did you let your Child be crucified on the cross? Was there no other way to show the depth of your love for us? Help us to understand. And help us to stop asking so many questions and to begin to go forward in life with what we do understand. Amen.

Monday

Expectations

Matthew 26:11–13—In remembrance of her
If we come to see the world in a certain way, if we believe that when A happens, B will always follow, then we close our lives off to God's desire for us to make changes. Stereotypes prevent us from seeing people as individuals. When we expect people to behave in certain ways, we set the stage for them to act only in those ways. If we say the poor will always be with us, that 6 percent will always be unemployed in an urban society, that some innocent people will always be sent to jail, why would we want to help them or try to improve the situation? We need to cut through the jungle of perceptions that tell us what we cannot do in order to see what is possible to do.

If we believe that God can do anything through us, then we will try to feed the hungry, comfort the lonely, heal the afflicted, and encourage the struggling. We will try to change the laws and the ways governments work in order to draw closer to justice for all people. We will become sojourners of faith in a land of endless possibilities. Do we expect enough of our faith? Or do we crumble in the face of so much adversity?

> Judge, most of the time we can delude ourselves into thinking that we are sufficient unto ourselves, that the plans we make will solve all our problems and make us happy. Then we walk out the door and encounter a world of other people with their own plans, trying to make themselves happy. We remember that it is not our plans that are real, but yours. If we can follow them, then we will be happy whether or not our plans succeed. Amen.

Tuesday

Tippy

Romans 8:38–39—Nothing can separate us
In a world accustomed to wars and violence, we have adjusted our perceptions so much that we take new reports of horrible suffering in stride, as a necessary part of modern life. We accept violence as the norm. To take time to slow down and pray, to be quiet for a while, to believe again that peace is the norm and that miracles do happen takes real courage, for it will transform our lives and make us look silly in the eyes of the world.

A number of years ago, a friend wrote that ever since she was a child, she had been awed by the way in which a caterpillar becomes a butterfly. As Tippy grew older, while her scientific understanding of the transformation grew, her sense of wonder remained undiminished. Then, over the years, as relatives and friends died—some tragically—the symbolism of the metamorphosis helped her find meaning and enabled her to reconcile the pain of her grief with the hope of her Christian faith.

She began to associate the emerging of the butterfly from the cocoon with Jesus' three days in the tomb, allowing her to understand something of the vast mystery of Jesus' death and resurrection. In the changing of Jesus' form and function, she came to believe that the new life of Easter morning really was possible—that death was only a passage to maturity.

When we are reborn as butterflies, after drying our wings in the warmth of the sun, we finally leave the ground and rise into the air to live a life we scarcely imagined before. In Tippy's understanding, death is simply, yet mysteriously, moving from the goodness of one world into the grandeur of the next. This is an imagery in which I, too, find much comfort.

Clouds reflecting off the lake.
Fish flying through the sky.
Pebbles laughing, cosmic jokes.
Do pebbles ever die?

Cattails growing along the shore.
Squirrels hiding food supplies.
Cocoons wrapped as winter's dead,
reborn as butterflies.

Hiking with my shadow,
wondering how wrens woo,
skipping pebbles off the clouds,
humming this hymn with you.

Mothering God, often we do not feel your love until we enact your love. We pray and study and ready programs of ministry to others, but you are so often silent in your approval. Then when we can wait no longer and put our plans into action, we discover you working beside us—guiding us, supporting us, and leading us into new areas of care. You had always been beside us, waiting for us to show faith and believe you when you said you would be with us always. Amen.

Wednesday

Goals and Desires

Philippians 3:12–14—I press on to make it my own
When we plan what we want from life, we decide on goals and formulate ways of reaching them. Often we choose to sacrifice something in

the present in order to reach something else in the future. We may do without vacations in order to make the down payment on a house. We may decide to work sixty-hour weeks for a couple of years in order to get our careers started. The danger with holding too fast to goals is that we sometimes sacrifice our present needs for goals that never come. Or we may find out, for example, that our careers will always demand sixty-hour weeks, and our work will end up consuming our lives.

To be with God in this moment is to open up all our plans to God's revisions, to listen for God's direction and make changes to fit God's needs. If we find ourselves saying that we can't respond to God now because we are working hard on something for God in the future, we cut ourselves off from God's presence in our current lives; we also reveal that we want to be in control, not God. We need, like Paul, to press on to make God's goals our own. We all say we want to be with God. We simply need to live as though this were true.

Like a father you discipline and nurture us, God. Like a mother you provide us with shelter and love. Like a parent who anticipates all our needs and even our dreams you guide us toward wholeness. Like a complete parent you allow us time and space to develop our uniqueness. Thank you for loving us. Amen.

Thursday

Emotions and Feelings

2 Samuel 22:2–7—God is my refuge
Christians have stored up a lot of guilt over prayer and the amount of time we spend with God. We feel we don't pray often enough, don't use the right words, or don't do it properly. We feel guilty if we don't enjoy praying. We may think we can bring only happy thoughts or only our needs before God; this leaves us feeling incomplete and frustrated because there's so much more to our lives that we want to share. We may even feel we aren't worthy of God's time, that we are such flawed human beings that God couldn't possibly care about our troubles or want to use us in ministry.

Our beliefs about proper Christian conduct and ethics often get in the way of exploring our faith and helping others in any way we can. But God works with us *where* we are and *as* we are. God brings us along as we learn to trust God's direction and ability to withstand anything we have to say. God is our refuge, in whose arms our hearts reside.

Word-made-flesh, it seems that the traits we hate in others are those that we don't want to acknowledge in ourselves. If only other people could be more wholesome! If only we could be so and not experience the cycle of disruptive behaviors that only serve our pride and greed. Life's pressures are not easy to withstand. Stay close to us, dear Jesus, and let us feel the movements of your dance. Amen.

Friday

Forsakenness

Psalm 22:1—"My God, my God, why have you forsaken me?"
Many who read the first line of this psalm will recall Jesus' words on the cross as recorded in Matthew 27 and Mark 15. There are a number of other parallels in Psalm 22: "All who see me mock at me" (7), "all my bones are out of joint" (14), "my mouth is dried up like a potsherd" (15), and "they divide my clothes among themselves" (18).

From the perspective of the writers of the Old Testament, the words of the psalmist speak of the dynamics of a common person trying to live a godly life in a society that doesn't value this, a society that sees misfortune as the result of sinfulness. Scorn, abuse, and persecution do happen to people who question society's values, in whatever age they live. These people, these martyrs of faith, hold true to the conviction they feel inside. And they complain to God about the abuse they receive: "O God, if I'm doing your work, then why am I suffering so much?" But that's the way things happen. If you're going to stand up for God and tell people that what they are doing is unethical, immoral, destructive, uncaring, or just plain stupid, there will always be those who will stand in your path and who will want to discredit and destroy you.

God of wanderers, do the voices that call for repentance also mention your call for justice? When we speak for you, do our voices prepare a path for others to walk toward you, or do we put up roadblocks? As wanderers who are homeless but who call everywhere "home," as people who are wounded and yet have been healed, as seekers who are hungry and thirsty but mostly for your Word, help us keep our eyes upon your holy mountain, that we may speak and work with compassion and not with judgment. Amen.

Saturday

Images of Jesus

Numbers 6:22–27—God's face will shine upon you
People have always interpreted Jesus for their own time and culture. This is to be expected. The presentation of Jesus in the New Testament—the most exacting record we have—resembles a collection of sketches more than it does a film documentary.

Mark wrote a bare-bones Gospel, presenting some facts and moving on. Matthew wrote for a Jewish audience, emphasizing concepts important to Jews—especially how Jesus was the fulfillment of long-awaited Jewish expectations. Luke wrote for a Gentile audience, downplaying Jesus' Jewishness and emphasizing how he reached out to include non-Jews. John wrote less about the details of Jesus' life than about what those details meant. Paul didn't write much about Jesus, either; he emphasized how Jesus was the answer to unfulfilled expectations in Mediterranean cultures. Each writer interpreted Jesus' life to maximize the Savior's impact on that writer's community.

Over the centuries, the images of Jesus have changed as people sought to connect Jesus with their lives, to affirm that God cares about what they are going through. These images have ranged from the personal to the grand, from the individual to the communal to the cosmic. How Jesus is presented in the media has also changed. Cecil B. DeMille's 1927 film *The King of Kings* portrayed an ascetic Christ, who did not eat or drink. The 1961 *King of Kings* featured a political Jesus. In 1965, he was a spiritual leader in *The Greatest Story Ever Told* and an angry prophet in *The Gospel According to St. Matthew. Jesus of*

Nazareth (1977) portrayed Jesus as the Messiah promised in the Scriptures. And *The Last Temptation of Christ* (1988) presented Jesus as a man who struggled with the reality of temptation.

Many movies, paintings, and other public images present Jesus as a fair-haired, blue-eyed European instead of someone born in the Middle East. This Jesus doesn't sweat in a land that is mostly desert; he appears emotionless in a society that tortures and kills its dissidents. We all carry images of Jesus with us that are central to our faith. We tend to see Jesus in certain ways because of specific needs in our lives.

One struggle Christians have always had is in deciding just how human and how divine Jesus was. Some people say, for example, that although Jesus drank wine, he didn't really like it. He ate food, but he preferred to fast. He associated with disreputable people, but only because he felt sorry for them. He laughed, smiled, and was witty in his parables, but he never told jokes. Often our human Jesus turns out to be a celestial being pretending to be human. On the other hand, some of us cast Jesus as someone who will always be there to rescue us from our mistakes, to clean up after us, as if God were our personal servant.

Images help us to understand something of the mystery of Jesus, although they can also get in the way. No single image will ever be inclusive enough to express the completeness of Christ Jesus. There aren't enough words in any language to describe all that Jesus is for everyone. God is beyond every attempt to define. The closer we get to God, the more we realize that all words and all images fall short of God's reality. But images do point us in the right direction, and they do help us to understand important things about Jesus. Fourth-century Christians put it well when they said, "We cannot know God by names, only by what God does."

O God, help us endure in our witness to the faith, never giving up or wavering in our conviction that you are a God of love who invites and heals, not a God of hatred who excludes and condemns. Help us love even the Pharisees and Sadducees of the church and all others who love laws more than they love you, who think that laws give them an insight into who is deserving of your love. Everyone is equally deserving—even they. Amen.

Community

Fifth Full Week in Lent

Yearning for Community

Acts 2:41–42—Welcoming God's message
No one can be in a spiritual community with others unless she or he can also be alone with God. The emphasis on solitude as a prelude to community is a reminder of Jesus' days alone in the desert before he began to live with and minister to others. Time alone renews our yearning for others.

When we come to faith, we come as individuals and profess "I believe." By professing, we join the community of faith. Communities sustain us, guide us, and challenge us to grow. Yet as there is a time to be in community, there is also a time to be by ourselves, praying, meditating on God's Word, and letting God work in the silences and activities of our daily lives. On Ash Wednesday, we acknowledged that we had drifted away from God and were longing to return home.

Being in a congregation is also a pilgrimage. Our goal is not for all of us to agree on everything, because we will continue to see things differently. The journey is to do things together, to share our perceptions, and thereby discover with one another who we all are and how God is working in the world through us.

Shepherd God, we believe that we are not alone in this life, that wherever we go, you are there with us—guiding us, supporting us, empowering us. There is no place we can go where you will not travel with us. Sometimes, though, we do not want to be guided or empowered by you. We want our lives to be predictable, with as few surprises and as little pain as possible. May we find the courage to follow wherever you lead, whatever the cost. This is our prayer. This is our only desire. Amen.

Monday

Objections to Community

1 Corinthians 1:4–9—Waiting for revelation
We find many reasons for not doing everything we can to further Jesus' work on earth: "I don't have enough time," "I'm barely scraping by as it is," "I need this job, unethical though it may be at times," "I'm not very talented," and so on.

I can imagine what the disciples were thinking in Jesus' last days, when he couldn't be talked out of going to Jerusalem and likely facing death. I can imagine all the excuses they found for not sticking around as Jesus was led away, tried, and executed. And I can imagine all their objections to putting themselves in danger to follow a dead leader— after all, he was dead.

Then Jesus rose and appeared to them, and all their confusions disappeared. They knew exactly what they were going to do and how they were going to do it. They got up, went right out, and spread the good news! No, they actually didn't. They still found reasons for keeping their faith hidden from the world until the day of Pentecost, when the Spirit came and touched them. Then what had been their confusion became their conviction.

Teacher God, sometimes your ways are like calculus—hard to understand, too abstract. At such times, we want to tell you to concern yourself with the real world. But it is in these times, when we are pushed beyond what we think we can understand, that we finally see beyond ourselves to glimpse part of you and your plans. This day, move us beyond our boundaries into your possibilities. Amen.

Tuesday

A Gifted Community

Romans 12:3–8—We have gifts that differ
We all have general abilities, and in life we tend to use these to get us through most everything. God, however, has given each of us specific talents and called us to use them in ministry—our passion in life. Joseph Campbell calls this "following our bliss." This is a scary thing for us to do, because most of the time we will have to stand alone to use these talents and then listen to the approval and disapproval of others. This is where community comes in. Our community can help identify our specific abilities and develop them so that we know how to use them. It can enable us to find ways of building ministries around our talents, and it can support us when we find the going difficult.

As we uncover and develop our passion in life, may we do so in "fear and trembling," that intriguing phrase that Søren Kierkegaard used. This is not the "fear" that if we mess up, God will zap us; rather, it is the awesome sense that the almighty and omnipotent God—the Creator of the universe—is the One who is personally asking us to do something. And it is "trembling" in the sense that we are taking this request very seriously, and we plan to do everything possible to ensure that our actions are acceptable to God. Our passion in life is not a hobby, not just something to do in our idle hours. It is our path to salvation.

Because God is revealed in every part of creation, every moment becomes sacred because we can encounter God at any time. But unless we are ready, we will not see.

Knowing that we are now new creatures, how do we express our being born again? By keeping ourselves *ready* to encounter each day, by *seeing* sparks of God's spirit all around us, and by *interacting* with the world, whether we feel we are ready or not.

"But how," you may ask, "can I stay ready?" These four steps will help.

1. Find your balance first thing in the morning. Do what you need to do to center yourself—whether it be taking a walk outside, praying, reading the Bible, writing to friends, practicing yoga, or something else.

2. Keep yourself ready to interact with the world. Get enough sleep and physical exercise, and eat right. Be mentally alert. Learn something new each day to maintain your curiosity. See something each day that awakens your spirituality, that makes your jaw drop in awe: Watch the sun rise. Listen to the ocean, if it's nearby. Watch a tall tree sway in the breeze. Walk inside a cathedral and marvel that such a thing can exist.

3. Look for God in everything and everyone around you. God is there.

4. When you see something of God, react. If you have found your passion, what you have seen will find expression there. If you haven't, then ask people who know you what they think your true gift is. Each of us needs to have a way to express his or her soul. It may be by creating something, by singing, painting, dancing, writing, or even talking with others. Only through these expressions do we discover and travel our roads to the promised land.

If we risk enough, if we put enough of ourselves on the line, we should feel a healthy sense of fear in the pit of our stomachs.

Martyr God, as you said in truth, a grain of wheat remains a solitary grain unless it falls into the ground and dies. But if it dies, it bears a rich harvest. Now my soul is in turmoil over the suffering in the world. What am I to do or say—"Save me from this hour"? No, let me go and live with the poor, doing what I can to relieve the misery and terror of daily life. What other thanks can I offer to you for my faith but to go to those whose hearts are broken, whose lives are troubled, and offer them the faith that I bear in Christ's name? Let me affirm that beyond the crushing of my life has begun an eternal alleluia, and from a thousand wounds of bodies and souls, a triumphant song! My arms may grow weary and my shoes may wear thin, but I will follow my God throughout the world! Amen.

Wednesday

Discovering Community

Mark 1:16–20—They left their nets and followed

There are a number of reasons why people come to church. Some want to get in touch with another reality. Some come for a centering in their lives, others for the companionship. A few come because that is how they were brought up, and this is the place to be on Sunday mornings. And some are here because this is the one place in the world that gives them hope.

Our sense of community begins with worship and is nurtured by our gatherings around the service—in the choir preparations, at coffee hour, in Sunday school, and in going out to lunch together afterwards. Some of us also gather during the week to pray together, study the Bible, work on social concerns, or simply talk. In all of these ways, we seek to share ourselves and learn more about how God is working in others and in the world.

We are called to seek the fullness of community by the nature of our faith.

Following Christ means leaving all behind in order to follow Jesus. It means giving up everything we possess in order that we may possess only Christ. In *The Good Book*, Peter Gomes asks, "What of the good life are we willing to give up that we might live a life that is good?" It is an appropriate question for our times. Community itself requires sacrifice.

Mostly, we are practical people and know that our personal resources allow us to do a world of good for others. Yet we also realize that our preoccupation with hanging on to our possessions often gets in the way of our doing more, of walking more simply with Jesus, of ministering more from our hearts than from our pocketbooks.

We seek to follow Jesus in all that we do, but sometimes we are not sure which path is the right one. Our community helps us to discern the path of love that moves through our hearts.

O God, we easily get caught up in the waterwheel of life. The faster life flows, the faster we turn, until we feel out of control. Slow us down so that we can affect life's moments as they pass. Help us think through what we are doing so we can see where our days are headed and redirect our lives if we are headed astray. Amen.

Thursday

The Church of the Saviour Community

Mark 5:18–19—Go home and tell others
During the time of the world wars and the intervening Great Depression, a concern for the social implications of faith was moving through the Christian church. There was also a growing interest in communal groups that would meet during the week and make faith personal. The Catholic Worker had been active for some time on the streets of New York, the Iona Community was formed in 1938, Taizé in 1940, and Koinonia in 1942. Inspiration and guidance for these groups came from people like Walter Rauschenbusch, Dietrich Bonhoeffer, and Peter Maurin, who felt that faith without works was dead and works without faith had no guiding principle to keep them on track.

In 1946, amid this climate of religious renewal, the Church of the Saviour was founded in Washington, D.C., under the direction of Gordon Cosby and dedicated to missionary activity. It aimed to find new ways of meeting people's needs in the communities in which they lived and to establish new structures for doing so. The church also asked much of those who wanted to be members. Each would have to make a commitment to spiritual discipline, stewardship, study, and involvement in a mission group. Elizabeth O'Connor has written extensively about the community's history and work.

In the years that followed, the ministry of the Church of the Saviour developed. Its mission groups responded to calls to share their lives with the poor, those recovering from addiction or abuse, at-risk children, refugees, the homeless, and with people with AIDS. From the beginning, the mission groups combined worship, prayer, and Bible study with their outward expressions of faith. Deeper faith and better-attuned ministries evolved together. The mission groups went into their neighborhoods knowing that their journeys outward were rooted in and nurtured by their journeys inward. Its mission continues today.

We confess to you, God of all people, that we have not taken seriously enough the burdens of peacemaking which you have placed upon us. Nor have we taken seriously enough the bond which you have proclaimed—that through you we are all sisters and brothers. We pray especially that the bond between the peoples of North America and Central America may be strengthened. Create in us new hearts— hearts of flesh and not of stone. Renew within us the desire to be peacemakers, people who express their faith through what they do. Amen.

Friday

What Is Community?

Romans 16:1–16—Greet your coworkers

I've found renewal of my Christian faith in a specific congregation. I had begun to think that organized religion was a sham, because I observed many congregations spending much of their time taking care of themselves and their own kind. Ethnic groups were often neglected until they left and formed their own congregations. But in this congregation, I found a place where people from all cultures and all continents were welcomed, participating, and worshiping. The congregation at Sunday worship wasn't monochromatic, it looked like rainbow sherbet. I found a diversity of convictions and opinions, a variety of economic situations and family structures, and a wide array of ministries. This congregation's diversity, while it continues to cause us growing pains, is one of our greatest strengths. Our variety of backgrounds and traditions is a treasure chest of wisdom and knowledge.

We struggle to understand one another at times, as we try to discern what new ministries God is leading us toward. This congregation is not confined to a legalistic structure that has a rule for every situation; it does not make decisions based on procedures but rather on need. Our tradition is to seek out new ways of sharing God's love in the world. This congregation fought for women's rights. It fought for African- and Asian- and Hispanic-American rights. It fought for peace in a time of war. And now it is fighting for gay/lesbian rights. This inclusivity and spunk are the reasons why I came here and why I stay.

There is an ongoing search for the gospel in our congregation, a search for the Spirit that keeps things moving, lest we settle into the comfort of the promised land, forgetting our God, forgetting the people still excluded from the sanctuary, and building a golden calf in our own likeness. "What does God require of us but to do justice, love kindness, and walk humbly with our God?" (Micah 6:8). For us, there is no turning back.

Suffering God, we know that when your people suffer, you suffer. We know that you have invited us to share in this suffering and challenged us to heal from our woundedness. O God, where there is hatred, let us bring reconciliation. Where there is oppression, let us come not just with words that inspire, but with actions that lead to justice.

Saturday

The Church in the Marketplace

Mark 10:46–52—The blind beggar at the crossroads

In my dream, I see the church surrounded by the daily market of the city, with coffee shops, arts-and-crafts booths, bookstores, and music stores dotting the neighborhood. The marketplace would be full of homegrown fruits and vegetables and handmade items. People would be interacting with one another as they buy and sell their goods, proudly showing one another what they have made. There would be fresh bread and hot soup, pottery and jewelry, paintings and woven textiles, the recitation of poems and the singing of songs that people have written this week. People would be milling about sharing thoughts and ideas. They'd be sitting on the church steps and at the outdoor cafés trading stories and dreams. Words of comfort as well as of challenge would be spoken, with sparks of inspiration shooting high above the multicolored banners of the many booths. Believers and nonbelievers would listen and learn from each other, community would expand. Faith would interact with society in this place where paths cross.

O God, make us strong so that we can continue the struggle for the equality and acceptance of all believers, a struggle begun by the elders and saints in our congregation. Let us not be distracted by the jackals and weasels of the church, who seek to box us in with lesser concerns. Amen.

$\mathscr{D}$eliverance

Holy Week

Yosemite Worship

Matthew 21:1–17—Jesus, the prophet
On this Sunday, Jews in Jerusalem are celebrating the Passover and their escape from slavery in Egypt long ago. They are enjoying their affluence and the festivities—the sights, the sounds, and all the wonderful aromas of different foods cooking. When Jesus comes along at the end of the Passover parade, riding on the back of a small donkey, they think it's a funny sight, and they cheer and lay down their cloaks before him. But only Jesus' followers recognize that something greater is going on than even they understand. Then Jesus goes to the Temple and drives out all those who are selling and buying. Those who are blind and lame come, and he heals them.

At first, it seems strange to be outdoors on Palm Sunday and not inside a church building singing hosannas. Yet being here makes me feel more connected with God. In church, I would imagine how hard Jesus' life was this week. I would think of the pain, the doubt, and the worry. Here I look up at the surrounding mountains and out over the meadows, and I feel God's presence and commitment to the world. I see life and death going on in a myriad of life forms. The notion of Jesus suffering affects me in the depth of my being. I feel the pain here; I would think about it in church.

There's little pretense in the valley. I don't worry about what to wear in order to worship God today. I'm going to wear the same clothing all day, and it will serve to keep me warm and dry. I won't put on different clothing in order to think about God, then take the clothing off and stop thinking. The thoughts and feelings I have will be for where I am with God, not for what others have planned for worship today. Worship is ongoing, happening throughout the day as nature breaks into my consciousness in many small moments. John Muir had similar thoughts: "I am sitting here . . . this Sabbath evening. I have not been at church a single time since leaving home. Yet this glorious valley might well be called a church, for every lover of the great Creator who comes . . . fails not to worship as never before."

Worship is a sustained feeling uninterrupted by the clock. Revelations appear one after the other, and God's presence is felt in deepening ways because of an openness to the unexpected.

I don't worry when this church service of the wild will begin or end, because it doesn't. I will be mindful of Palm Sunday all day. There will be no ushers except the squirrels who invite me off on new adventures; there will be no pastors to say "Let us now begin our worship." The morning psalms of the birds have already done that. I suspect I will also feel closer to the crucifixion later this week because I am outdoors where it happened. In the waving of the trees in the breeze today, I see a holy procession.

Entering Yosemite Valley, I am full of anticipation. When I catch my first glimpse of El Capitan glowing in the early morning light, my heart leaps with joy. I park the car quickly and walk among the oak trees smelling the heady scents of the Sierra. I wander around on paths that wind through the quietness of the valley, trying to absorb as much as I can. What will you teach me this trip, O God? How will you lead me deeper into your mystery?

Monday

Pilgrimage

Matthew 21:18–23:39—Jesus, teller of parables
In the morning, Jesus returns to Jerusalem. A fig tree with no fruit withers at his command. The chief priests throw questions at him all day as to his authority to preach and heal, and Jesus answers in parables. Later, on the Mount of Olives, Jesus' disciples ask him when his reign will begin. Jesus says that first the Human One must be handed over to be crucified.

Over the centuries, it has been a tradition for Christians to undertake a pilgrimage to Palestine for Holy Week. They wanted to be where Jesus had been in order to capture more of the feeling of his last days and to draw closer to the power of God's presence.

Our pilgrimage is to become free of our expectations of God, free of dreams, desires, and stereotypes of how we should pray and what we should expect in return. When we are free of our own self-condemnation and even our reluctance to be known as Christians, then we are open to God's movement in our lives. Morning prayer becomes a time of excitement, of wondering what God has in store for us today. This opens up a place of wildness, of untamed vitality. By having no plans that can't be changed, no desires that we don't allow God to provide for or decline, no expectations but to meet God in every moment, and no limits on how God can appear, then we begin to see God in every face and to do God's work in every step we take. We begin to share God's compassion with others through everything we do and every word we speak. Even a glance from our eyes can convey God's love.

Journeys of pilgrimage offer us a time to find the presence we long for, a time of preparing to meet our part of the covenant. On a rocky island called Iona off the western coast of Scotland, on the Incan trail leading up to holy places in the Andes Mountains, along the pilgrimage trails in southern Japan, we step away from our daily lives and intentionally seek what we value most. With a purity of intention and few distractions, we discover the reality of presence that touches us.

To be on a walk of pilgrimage, a journey into the heart of God, is to live without expectations, without needs or guilt; to move beyond the limitations of traditions or goals, even beyond the handiness of words; to not think about doing but simply to do and to let God empower, guide, and speak through us as we go. This is a journey that continues beyond Lent.

Quiet pervades the camp as people get ready for the day's activities. Some are reading in their sleeping bags; some are preparing their equipment for climbing or hiking; others are stretching. Some have wandered down to the river to write in their journals, trying to find words to explain yesterday's experiences. What is it that we seek, God? We are not here just for exercise or thrills. We seek to touch life directly, to push ourselves right to the edge of our abilities, that we may see what lies just beyond. Be with us when we reach this place of uncertainty, that we may see without fear and hold on to what we do not yet understand. Amen.

Tuesday

Jack and Weasel

Matthew 24:1–26:5—Jesus, a teacher
It is two days before the Passover. The chief priests and scribes gather to figure out a way to get rid of Jesus.

Jack and Weasel were out one day secretly causing confusion. They liked to do this frequently because then everyone had to come to them to find out what was going on. (They also got to be treated with respect, which they couldn't manage by being themselves.)

Coyote came along and said, "Now boys, you shouldn't be causing so much trouble. You're the town leaders, and you're getting everyone riled up about nonsense."

"You're one to talk!" Jack said. "You break all the rules. And you have no standards; you accept everyone. At least we're unifying the town!"

Coyote replied, "But I don't do it for myself. I do it so that everybody will know what's going on. And I don't hide my intentions. You hide behind your rules and make wounds fester until they infect every-one. If only you had something to offer."

"Oh, but we do," Weasel piped in. "We offer order and decency."

"Order and decency?" Coyote cried. "You set the town against itself, fabricating illusions and replacing the foundation of goodness with nothing but fear. But I think you do have a place among us—there by the side of the road with your cousin, Hyena. There you can sit and be a reminder to all who pass by that behind your false smiles are animals with vicious jaws."

Unshakable God, when we experience the shaking of what we have always thought to be secure, we are overwhelmed. We lose our bear-ings, and it seems as if there's nothing left to hold on to. We also live in the fear of a spiritual earthquake. We have trouble believing that all things hold together in Christ, no matter what happens. O God, relieve our disbelief. Amen.

Wednesday

Suffering

Matthew 26:6–16—Jesus, the good news
Every day Jesus is teaching the people in the Temple. Many people get up early in the morning to listen to him talk. While at the house of Simon the leper, a woman comes up to Jesus, breaks open a jar, and pours costly ointment over his head. The disciples object, but Jesus says that she is doing what she can for him while there is still time. In the evening, he goes out and spends the night on the Mount of Olives.

The snow starts falling while I am sitting by the river. The birds splashing in the water along its edges don't seem to take notice, unless they begin to play with a little more excitement. The large flakes quickly cover the landscape, sticking to rocks and trees, unifying every-thing under a common blanket of white. My thoughts turn from the snowstorm to the Ahwanechee, who used to live in this valley. Did they gather inside during storms like this to share stories, traditions, and concerns?

I think of the suffering that Jesus went through during his last week, and then of friends and their struggles—with cancer, HIV, epilepsy, poverty. I sense that if we all lived here, our sorrows would not strike as deeply because our expectations would be simple—to live this day as best we can. The anguish over lost dreams wouldn't matter as much because we would be focused on today. Living in harmony with nature, our basic needs of food and shelter would be available. Friends and family would be close at hand.

Black Hawk, chief of the Sauk and Fox, spoke of this sense of community: "We always had plenty; our children never cried from hunger. The Rock River furnished us with an abundance of excellent fish, and the land being very fertile, never failed to produce good crops of corn, beans, pumpkins, and squashes. "

The call of a Steller's jay brings my thoughts back to the storm. I must have been thinking for some time, for now I'm covered by two inches of snow and I blend into the landscape. Since I'm warm enough, I sit still for a while longer, to see if one of the birds will land on me.

Stone God, who dwells in mighty cathedrals and tiny chapels, we come to be with you for a while—to rest in your presence, to let our hearts and minds wander around in your place, to suspend our disbelief and believe that here, for now, we are with you and everything is all right.

In soaring cathedrals that raise our eyes ever upward, with climbing gray pillars, flying buttresses, and large sweeping movements of stone; with stained-glass windows that shine through our eyes and into our hearts with bright bursts of colors; where the chant of evensong echoes for hours, first in the vast open stretches as it rises into the upper air, joining the faint sounds of centuries still resonating in the stone, and then into the depths of our minds—here we deal with matters of conversion.

It is not a feeling of being overwhelmed by the size of the place but of being part of something beyond our own dimensions. Every movement I make sounds out an echo as if to say, "I am noticed, I do matter even in this grand place. I am part of the great multitude of believers that has been coming here over the centuries to be with you, an almighty, eternal God. I share something with the martyrs of the faith buried here."

In tiny chapels tucked into neighborhoods, half-hidden now by bushes and trees, their stones stained with the passage of time, providing room for only a dozen worshipers, the space is intimate, dark, and quiet. A single candle illuminates the shadows. Here one feels the presence of a personal God. Here the individual prayers of past generations have accumulated on the walls like the dark soot from the candles. Every sound is quickly absorbed, as if my presence is all that matters. Here I face God directly, presence to presence, and work out the details of my faith. The stone at the altar where I kneel has been worn down from generations of people kneeling to pray. In chapels, I work out the meaning of my faith.

O God, forgive me for needing to see you on a grand scale as well as on intimate terms, for you are everything to me, and I need to see you in everything if I am to believe fully. Everything I find noble and good, I want to be yours. Every image, every created thing, every living creature, every word that moves and lifts my heart, I want to know comes from you. Thank you, Almighty God and my closest Companion, for being in all the places where I travel.

Maundy Thursday

Table Sharing

Matthew 26:17–75—Jesus, a servant
On the evening of the Passover, Jesus gathers with his disciples, breaks bread with them, pours a cup of wine, and says, "This is my body and my blood. Remember." He washes their feet as an example. Then they go out to the Mount of Olives, where Jesus is arrested because of Judas's good intentions. The disciples scatter.

Gathered around the table with Jesus were the disciples. They had come into the group with different agendas and with different expectations of what the next few years would bring. Some were looking for heavenly glory. The old zealots were hoping for a military insurrection. But Jesus kept pushing ahead in his own way. His determined entrance into Jerusalem on Sunday only seemed to lead to a death that did not make sense to them. But they had survived the parade and the Temple uproar, and now they were feasting.

As Jesus was telling them once more that his way was the way of a servant, that they would eat his body and drink his blood, the disciples leaned together into interest groups, as da Vinci's *Last Supper* pictures it, to ask one another, "What's he doing?" "What does he mean?" They did not understand how their dreams fit into Jesus' plans. Later on, one of them would slip out and try to force Jesus into action. Still later, the rest of them would slip away, protecting their self-interests. The disciples had a nice social group going, but they weren't pulling together. They weren't a community yet. That would come later, when each of them decided that he only needed one dream to guide him—Jesus' dream.

Sometimes I feel that way about our congregation: we have a nice relationship going, but real community exists only in our special interest groups. We coordinate efforts between groups, but we don't often empower the whole congregation with a single vision. We tolerate and open our doors, but we don't work at getting into one another's hearts.

A while back, I participated in a year-long prayer and Bible study group with other church members. We came from different backgrounds and had different interests. We met during the week in one another's homes and shared what had happened to us over the last week. We learned the details of one another's lives. We listened, we supported one another, we read Scripture and prayed together. Since then, even though we are no longer meeting together, a feeling of community has lingered among us. This experience has left me wanting more.

When we break the bread and share the juice together, we are not just saying that we all belong to Jesus Christ, we are also saying that we belong to one another, to all the other members of our congregation. We are saying, in essence, that we are willing to "pour it all out," as Jesus had done for his disciples.

Strengthen us to endure in our witness to the faith, O God, never giving up or wavering in our conviction that you are a God of love who invites and heals, not a God of hatred who excludes and condemns. Help us love even the Pharisees and Sadducees of the church and all others who trust laws more than they trust you. Amen.

Good Friday

Who Crucified Jesus?

Matthew 27:1–61—Jesus, the crucified
In the morning, Jesus is led before Pilate, who asks him why he should not be put to death for inciting the people to riot. Jesus does not answer; he is led away, beaten, crucified, and laid in a tomb. The disciples are nowhere to be found. A few women keep watch.

The Romans, who carried out the execution, crucified Jesus. They were trying to keep the political situation under control. They had the *power,* so they used it for their own goals. Also the Jewish leaders, who demanded his death, crucified Jesus. They were trying to keep the religious situation under control. They had the *authority,* so they used it for their own purposes. Also the disciples, who ran away instead of standing up for Jesus. They were trying to keep their personal lives under control. They had personal and family *responsibilities* to think about, so they crucified him. The members of each group used whatever means they had to keep their lives under control, so that they wouldn't have to respond to something that would change their lives.

In this century, we've witnessed the death camps of Auschwitz and Bergen-Belsen; the police dogs and fire hoses of Birmingham; the white handprint of the disappeared in El Salvador; the ethnic cleansings in Bosnia, Rwanda, Iraq, and Tibet. And we think, "That's so sad. Why doesn't somebody do something to help them?" As Martin Niemoeller concluded as group after group was taken away to the Nazi death camps, "If we don't speak up against injustice whenever it happens to anybody, no one will be left to speak up when they come to take us away." One day we will reach the point, as at Stonewall, where we will say, "The injustice stops here."

We crucify Jesus when we value stability over growth in individuals, security of our possessions over community needs, our comforts over sharing with those who are suffering, and the quick fix instead of educating for long-term change. We choose Barabbas over Jesus each year when we refuse to follow Jesus wherever he leads, at whatever the cost.

We choose Barabbas when we choose self-interests over mission, we choose death over life, and we crucify our claim to being followers of Jesus.

God-with-us, is it a lack of courage that keeps me from walking with you? Or is my vision clouded over? It is time to see you clearly, time to walk with you along your path, time to walk in your light. It is high time to be disciplined and cease doing what dissipates my energies, drains my dreams, and destroys my love. It is time to come fully awake, to walk without stumbling, to run without fading! But, O God, help me begin by first learning to walk. Amen.

Holy Saturday

Waiting: Yosemite Vigil

Matthew 27:62–66—Jesus is not here
The chief priests and Pharisees come before Pilate and remind him that Jesus said he would rise from the dead in three days. Guards are posted around the tomb. The disciples secretly gather indoors, waiting for the knock on the door.

The crucifixion is over. The disciples have scattered and are now hiding. They do not know whether they dare to believe what Jesus said was true: that he would rise on the third day and be with them again. If he does not rise, then they can go home, resume their lives, and wistfully remember a special time. If he does come back, they know that their lives will be changed forever and that there will be no turning back ever again. So on this Saturday they wait, not knowing what to hope for. Although it would be hard for a time, it would be easier if Jesus stayed dead and the journey ended.

But something inside them says that it doesn't matter one way or the other. Something inside wouldn't let them set aside the last three years anyway. Something inside would get them back on the road, traveling and sharing the good news with people they've never met. They know this because, as they wait, they discover that Jesus has fulfilled their hearts' dreams.

This night we also relive the anxiety of the disciples, wondering if Jesus will rise from the dead tomorrow. We gather tonight to remember how God has been with us in our troubles and joys since the beginning. We gather to prepare for the fulfillment of God's promise in the dawning of Easter morning.

In the cool of the evening, as darkness wraps its cloak of peace around the shoulders of the mountains, as the sun slowly separates the sky into bands of glowing colors, I go out once more for a walk. As I move along the path, each step releases some tension and the day eases into perspective. With each step, a gathering calm renews my hope. After my own thoughts have been shared, my mind opens to the Other. As the stars begin to come out, each step draws me closer to my beloved, my God. The thoughts of Peter van Breemen, in his book *As Bread That Is Broken*, call me further into God's presence: "We eat a piece of bread. The bread becomes part of us. It rises to new life. Prayer transforms us into bread that is broken, and like bread we are consumed in the gift of ourselves to others."

I walk on in the dark without knowing where I am headed—savoring this feeling, reveling as the falling dew releases the scents of the night—pine, bay laurel, and marsh marigold. I hear the murmuring of the Merced River flowing by in the dark toward the San Joaquin Valley. I feel the zest of the night breeze on my face. I am being made whole! If only this time, this walk, this night could have no benediction. If only I could stay here, in this openness of prayer. This vigil is a point of stillness, the place around which the rest of my life will revolve.

Song of Zion, we believe that you will come and strengthen the weak, will bring down the mighty, will restore righteousness to its place. But we are feeling broken and oppressed, and we are tired of waiting and suffering. We're tired of believing when so much hardship keeps coming down upon us: unending poverty, AIDS and cancer, earthquakes and hurricanes. Help us not become depressed. Help us believe. Help us wait with hope until your time comes. Amen.

$\mathcal{R}$esurrection

Easter Week

Easter Sunday

Easter Dawn

Matthew 28:1–20—Go and make disciples
Before dawn on Easter morning something wakes me. I crawl out of my sleeping bag into the near-freezing air and stiffly amble out into the meadow that nestles in the center of the valley. Around me the snow-capped mountains rise from the valley floor to stretch ten thousand feet into the still-dark sky and toward the stars. The moonlit walls of the valley look like a pair of hands offering up the valley as a gift for the wounded of the cities. In the peacefulness that surrounds me, the feeling that I do not need to fear anything becomes almost palpable.

The frost on the milkweed twinkles in the starlight. The deer rise from their beds in the meadow to eat the breakfast provided for them by the oak trees. The mountains catch the first rays of dawn and glow with God's light. Pines stand proudly before the morning sky with God's glory sparkling in their branches. All is right with the world in this creation of a new day!

Within me a strong sense of adoration and thankfulness surges up toward whoever it is who is loving me, who is loving this valley. Seldom do I feel adoring of much, especially of an omnipotent Creator, but now in the pervading silence of this moment, all I can do is let this feeling of worship flow. I feel rooted and swept away at the same time.

O God, my Light and my Salvation;
whom shall I fear?
O God, the Stronghold of my life,
heal me and guide me;
set me high upon a rock, that I might see your light,
feel your salvation in the beating of my heart
and in the work of my hands. (Based on Psalm 18)

God-burning-inside-us, gather us together in our needs, that we no longer may be diffuse in our energies or distracted by unimportant and compulsive matters. Touch us with your fire. Ignite our dead coals, that love may burst forth again into flame, providing heat enough to warm those who are cold and light enough to illuminate the path of compassion. Amen.

Monday

In the Days to Come

Luke 24:13–35—Along the road
On Easter morning, Jesus first appeared to a group of women. Later, he appeared before the gathered disciples. Still later, he was seen walking with a couple on the way to Emmaus. Although each of us needs to face our risen Savior individually, we first find our place in faith, undoubtedly, as part of a community. And from our community, we discern revelations about Jesus that we would not have discovered on our own.

In the days after Easter, the disciples and the other followers formed communities to sustain the movement and their ministries. As they went out into the far corners of the world, they knew that they had a base of support back home. Sometimes they took with them money for the journey; sometimes, the companionship of friends along the way; but they always set out from home with prayers and guidance for the difficult times. This journey is also our own, and it begins anew every morning.

Let me wake this morning, God, and every morning, with you in my thoughts. Let me feel your touch and hear your voice speaking words of assurance and challenge. When I leave my home today, and every day in the years to come, let me sense you walking beside me, guiding me. Let me seek to speak only with your wisdom and act only with your compassion. Help me to leave behind my security of faith and say "yes" to all the unknown challenges that come my way. I so look forward to joining you on your pilgrimage throughout the world. Let me pack a small bag, and we can begin our journey. Amen.

Index of Meditations

Index of Prayers

Index of Scripture References